THE DREAM CATCHER

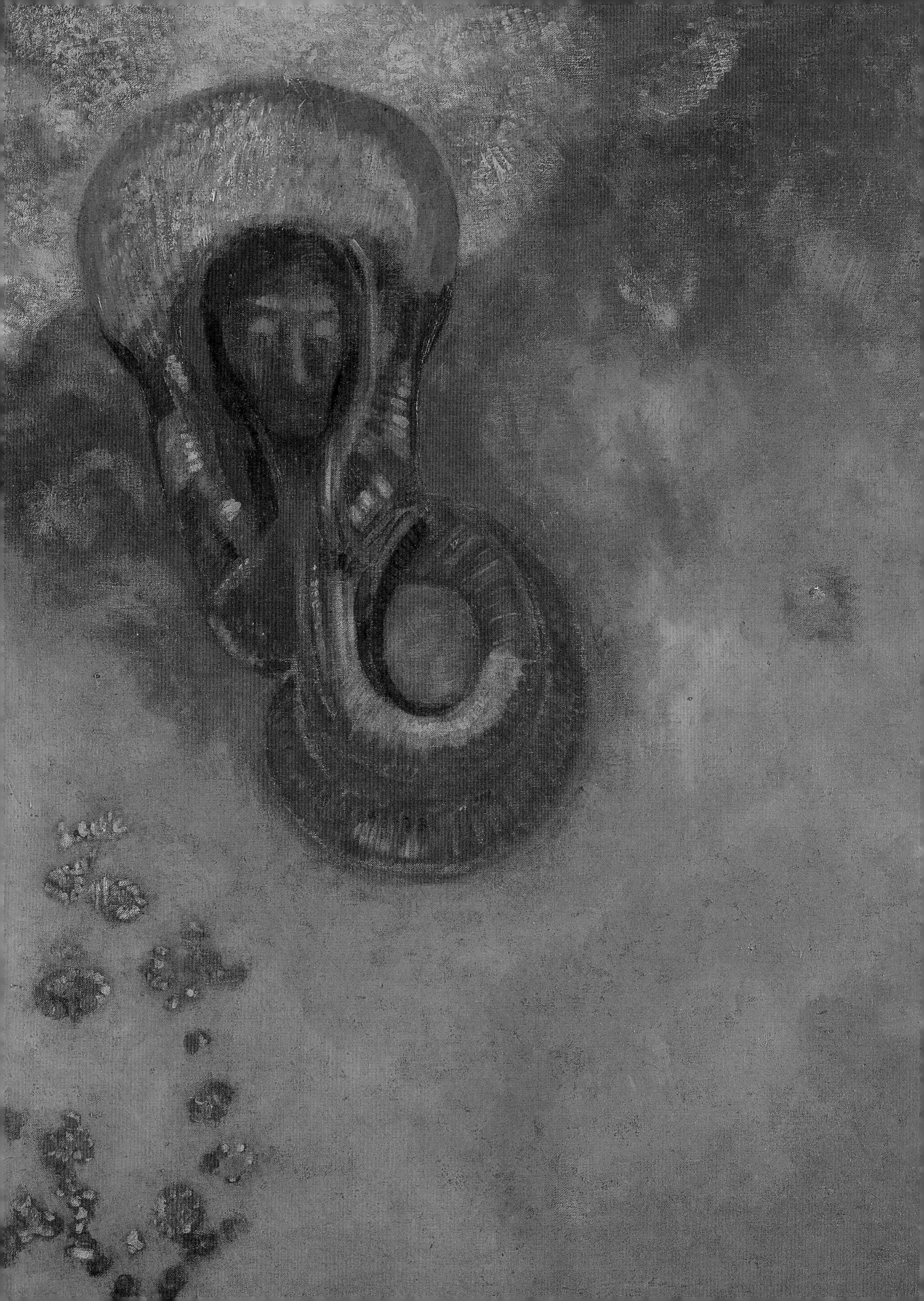

THE

DREAM CATCHER

Unravel the Mysteries of your Sleeping Mind

lori reid

ELEMENT

Shaftesbury, Dorset ❖ Rockport, Massachusetts ❖ Melbourne, Victoria

Published in Great Britain in 1997 by
Element Books Limited
Shaftesbury, Dorset SP7 9BP

Published in the USA in 1997 by
Element Books Inc.
PO Box 830, Rockport, MA 01966

Published in Australia in 1997 by
Element Books Limited
and distributed by Penguin Australia Ltd.
487 Maroondah Highway, Ringwood, Victoria 3134

Designed and created with the
The Bridgewater Book Company

Element Books Limited
Editorial Director: Julia McCutchen
Managing Editor: Caro Ness
Project Editor: Allie West
Production Director: Roger Lane
Production: Sarah Golden

The Bridgewater Book Company
Art Director: Peter Bridgewater
Designer: Angela Neal
Managing Editor: Anne Townley
Picture Research: Vanessa Fletcher
Studio photography: Ian Parsons
Illustrations: Grace Crivellaro, Ivan Hissey

Printed and bound in Singapore
British Library Cataloguing in Publication data available

ISBN 1 85230 998 9

CONTENTS

HOW TO USE THIS BOOK

The Dream Catcher kit is designed to help you unlock the hidden meaning of your dreams. There is a blank journal for you to keep beside your bed in which you can record your dreams, and, in the second part of the kit, an accessible guide to understanding your dreams. Recording your dreams will make them easier to interpret, so that you can begin a process of self-discovery during which you will also develop a greater understanding of those around you.

HERBS FOR HEALTHY SLEEP

"Lettuce," wrote Nicholas Culpeper, the great seventeenth-century English physician and herbalist, "gently disposes the patient to sleep." In further extoling the virtues of this herb, he tells us that it also has the power to "repress venereous dreams."

Herbal Pillow
You can make a herbal pillow or bath sachet by following the instructions on pages 46–47

Chamomile

Lettuce apart, herbalists have recognized the healing properties of plants since ancient times. Indeed, herbs have always played a large role in medicine, and folk remedies have been handed down for centuries from one generation to the next. The recent expansion in the market of herbal teas testifies not only to the perennial popularity of herbal preparations, but also to our continuing belief in their health-giving effects.

Giant among the herbs containing a soothing and sedative agent is chamomile. This is a gentle herb which can be infused and drunk as a tea before bedtime to aid restful sleep. Others with similar sleep-inducing

dried herbs for relaxing sleep

- Chamomile – to promote sleepiness
- Rosemary – to relieve stress and induce happy dreams
- Lemon balm – to calm the nerves
- Sage – to ensure long life
- Lavender – to reduce tension and for its fragrance
- Thyme – for its sedative properties
- Marjoram – to open the airways and speed up healing
- Woodruff – to aid relaxation

44

suggested aids for peaceful dreaming

RHYTHMS OF SLEEP

Whether you are an insomniac or the sort of person who goes out like a light the minute your head touches the pillow, once you have dropped off, research shows that your sleep will follow a set pattern. For the first ten minutes you will drift in a twilight world, held beween consciousness and unconsciousness. Slowly, you begin to sink deeper and deeper, until you are at your most relaxed, and as far away from wakefulness as sleeping will allow.

Reaching this stage of deep sleep takes roughly forty-five minutes, after which you begin to reverse the journey, climbing up again to the top levels of lighter sleep. In all, the sinking and rising form a wave pattern that takes some ninety minutes to complete and which then repeats itself over and over again, sometimes four, five, even six times throughout the night, depending on the duration of sleep.

Specific physical changes accompany the sleep cycle. In deep sleep, brain activity is reduced, blood pressure drops, and our breathing slows down. At this stage we lose muscle tone, our limbs are heavy, and our bodies are in a state similar to paralysis. Chemical changes also take place now. Growth hormone, secreted from the pituitary gland, enables the body to grow and the tissues to repair themselves.

But it is during the lighter phases of sleep that most of our dreaming takes place. As we rise out of deep sleep, blood-flow to the brain begins to increase, as does brain activity. At this point, both our breathing and pulse rates become erratic and blood pressure begins to rise. Our eyes begin to move around beneath our closed eyelids as if we were watching a film on a screen, and it is this, known as rapid eye movement, or REM, that shows we are dreaming. Our muscles are still deeply relaxed, presumably to disable us from acting out our dreams.

Wave pattern
Deep and lighter sleep phases alternate, like ocean waves, throughout the night

fascinating facts about sleep

- In an average lifetime we spend in the region of twenty-five years asleep.
- Old wives' tales that encourage us to get our beauty sleep are not far off the mark, since it is while we sleep that our bodies heal and repair themselves.
- The amount of sleep each person needs varies with the individual. The average requirement is around six or seven hours, although some people cannot cope with fewer than ten.
- The duration of sleep we require also varies at different times in our lives. Babies sleep almost continuously through the day and night. However, adults need less and less sleep as they get older. Elderly people sleep least of all.

17

Left: **Part 1 of this book, Sleeping and Dreaming Explained, shows the importance of dreams for human civilization throughout the centuries, and how research in the last hundred years has greatly advanced our understanding of dreaming.**

clear explanation of the processes of sleeping and dreaming

listing of fascinating facts

Left: **The dream journal is designed to help you keep a record of your dreams.**

fill in the date and time of your dream

space to record the details and images of your dreams

advice on getting a good night's sleep

Above: **This is a spread from Part 2, Aids to Restful Sleep and Peaceful Dreaming. This section of the book describes how best you can prepare yourself to sleep well and remember your dreams through the use of herbs, essential oils and gemstones.**

Right: **Part 3 of the book, The Key to your Dreamworld, is a comprehensive guide to the images and themes in your dreams. It includes an extensive index.**

the dream catcher

loved ones and important events

FUN AND FESTIVITIES

Parties, celebrations, and having fun with our friends and family are all occasions that can raise the spirits. Laughter, we now recognize, has enormous therapeutic value, providing a tonic that can instantly lift our moods and make us feel physically as well as psychologically better.

Frivolity *Dancing shows your life is full and busy*

Judging from our dreams, the unconscious mind, too, it would appear, enjoys a sense of humor. It likes using puns in our dreams, amusingly presenting us with information that can be interpreted on any number of levels, or else it teases us by wrapping the message around a play on words. Indeed, a dream that is being recounted all too often sounds like something straight out of comedy, or more suited to the theater of the absurd.

It is as well to bear this in mind when analyzing your dreams, but especially so when dealing with those that contain images of entertainment. For, among the more sententious dream symbolism, we must not miss the fact that dreams can also provide a strong element of fun.

BIRTHDAY PARTIES

Are you a guest or the host at this party? Is it lively, full of music and laughter, or does it resemble more of a wake? Dreaming that you are a sparkling host or hostess surrounded by a large group of people, either confirms your popularity or, depending on the context, may be a wish-fulfillment dream highlighting how much you dearly wish you had lots of friends. Happiness, too, may be interpreted both ways, according to your own personal circumstances, either reflecting your own contentment in life, or as a compensation for the sadness you are experiencing. The emotions you feel on waking will provide the key.

On a different level, because birthdays mark a turning point, the message may be one of new beginnings when they feature in a dream, pointing out the end of a particular phase in the dreamer's life and the start of a new one. Dancing and activity at the party could reflect that you have hit a busy time in your life at present, but, since it is at a party, it implies that your efforts are bringing you a good deal of pleasure and satisfaction. If there is a birthday cake, take note of the number and color of the candles because these, too, could be carrying information significant to the interpretation of the dream.

70

WEDDINGS

Weddings symbolize a union or a merger. Or they may represent the coming together of two people or of two states of being, opposite yet complementary to each other. Such a dream as this, for example, may reflect a business partnership. On a higher level, it may signify the union of conscious and unconscious, or the fusion of the rational with the creative. Alternatively, dreaming of a wedding may be a reminder of other kinds of vows that have been taken and promises that have been made. For single people particularly, the image of a wedding may constitute a wish-fulfillment dream.

RELIGIOUS FESTIVALS

The excitement and anticipation of presents may well induce youngsters to dream about festivals such as Christmas. But behind these times of celebration lies a religious theme that prompts the dreamer to consider the spiritual side of life.

Diwali or Candlemas, however, by introducing the element of light, might signify a breakthrough, a solution to a problem: in short, "seeing the light." Other dreams of celebration, such as Rosh Hashanah or the Chinese Spring festival, which mark the start of the new year, may, like dreams about birthdays, symbolize new beginnings.

71

detailed interpretations of dream subjects and images

divided into sections and sub-sections to help you find what you are looking for

part one

SLEEPING AND DREAMING EXPLAINED

YOUR WORLD IN A DREAM

Let's put our cards on the table. You are the only person who can accurately analyze your own dreams. You are the only person who is in full possession of all the facts and all the memories, who has lived through all the events and experienced all the sights and sounds and emotions that contribute to the stories in your dreams. You are the only one who talks your own language, thinks your own thoughts, feels your own passions. Through living your life, you have made up your own shorthand to describe what you see, and your own personal codes to understand your world. How, then, can anyone enter your mind and tell you what your dreams mean? The truth is, no one can. This is something you must learn to do for yourself and The Dream Catcher *will help you do just that.*

Common themes
Right: Water is one of the most commonly dreamt-of subjects or images

Sunny days
Far right: Sunny scenes in your dreams are a sign of creative expression

LABYRINTHS OF YOUR MIND

Your dreams are personal to you. They are part of you because they come from inside your own mind. They contain messages from your unconscious, that part of your mind that holds memories and impressions but which you cannot get at when you are awake because the information is so deeply buried in the labyrinths of your mind.

When you are asleep, however, your unconscious mind becomes active, and that is when you dream. All the dreams that you have are made up of your own experiences, things that you pick up with your senses – how you see, hear, and smell the world around you, how things taste to you, and how the environment feels through your own fingertips.

For each one of us, those experiences, which turn into our memories and impressions, are made up of associations linking those events with particular feelings and sensations. Often we tend to condense those experiences into one single vivid representative symbol – a smell, taste, color – which, at another time in our lives, has the power to convey us back to that moment and allows us to relive in our mind's eye that event, which may have taken place yesterday, or last week, or in the distant past of our childhood days.

What does it mean?

Right: The correct interpretation of your dream will depend upon your personality and what is happening in your life

Here, then, is what our dream images are made of. An association of experiences and feelings encapsulated in each symbol, or "a world in a grain of sand."

It is precisely because our images or symbols are packed with so much meaning in this way that it is sometimes difficult to interpret our dreams. What is more, because of our individual experiences and associations in life, the same symbol can bring to mind different things to different people. The image of a clock in your dream, for example, may take you back to an important examination, when you were working against time to answer the questions, the ticking of the clock in the school hall contributing to the pressure you were under. For someone else, however, who yesterday bought a clock for his or her parents' golden wedding anniversary, dreaming of this image will convey emotions of quite a different kind.

To understand your dreams, then, you must follow the labyrinths of your mind. Some dreams will be easy to decipher. Those that are not will require you to take each symbol and consider what it means to you, what memories it conveys, what associations it opens up before you, and what feelings it brings back into your life. Each image will have the potential to take you along many routes, the majority of which will turn out to be blind alleys. When you find the correct

road, however, you will know you have taken the right direction because the associations and the feelings will simply fall into place and feel right, and the meaning of your dream will suddenly become crystal clear.

A single dream image may have several possible associations, each of which has its own cluster of related memories, leading you through a sequence of linked experiences from your life.

LEVELS OF MEANING

Your unconscious mind is not only ingenious, it also has a sense of humor! It talks to you in your dreams using the language of riddles, heaping puns on top of metaphors, and toying with words and their meanings in such a way that would make the most complex cryptic crossword seem like child's play. On top of that, it flouts all laws of time and space and continuity, wrapping levels of interpretation inside more levels of interpretation so that meanings can be peeled off as one might peel off skin after skin of an onion. Profound statements are clothed in mundane observations. Obvious solutions are disguised in elaborate imagery. Symbols, whether part of your own private language or of wider universal significance, abound.

STATING THE OBVIOUS

Dreams consist of a series of images or word-pictures. Some you can interpret at face value, but others require a little lateral thinking; you may need to recognize that a pun or a play on words is being used. For example, if yesterday you stood looking out of the kitchen window at your son in the back yard as he chopped wood for the fire, the following night you might dream about your family settling down to their supper while a nice pile of logs burns happily in the living room grate. A basket of logs, newly chopped with the ax-marks still clearly visible, stands in readiness by the side of the fireplace.

Here, then, is a factual dream, replaying an event that took place in your life just prior to this dream. In the dream you see your family – in waking life you were watching your son, who is, naturally, a member of this family. You are all eating your supper – remember

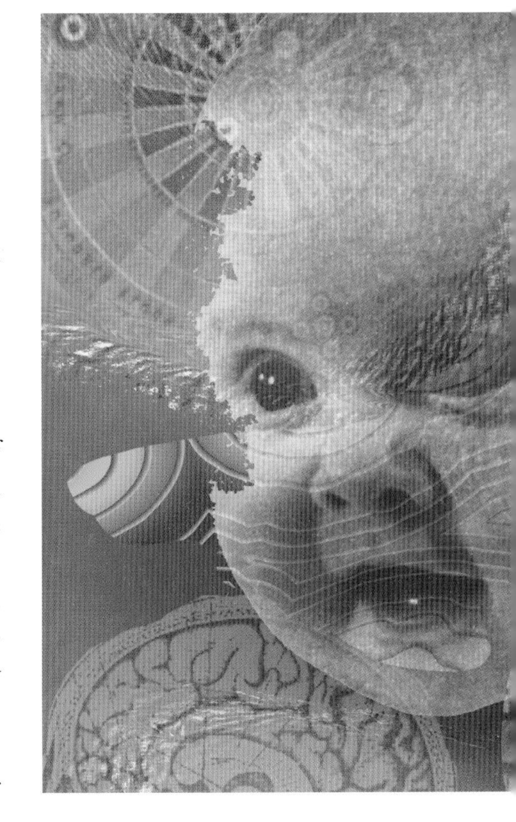

yesterday you were standing in the kitchen, the place where food is prepared, so this is an obvious link with the supper. In the dream, you see the logs in the basket – these were the logs your son was chopping in the yard.

ADDING THE METAPHORS

If you were to wake up and remember this dream, the connection between its contents and the events of yesterday will seem quite apparent to you. But wait a moment or two and take another look at some of these images. Look again at the basket of logs, look at the ax-marks showing the little chunks of wood that have been hacked out. Why does your dream draw your attention to the basket of logs, and in particular to the chipped surface of the wood?

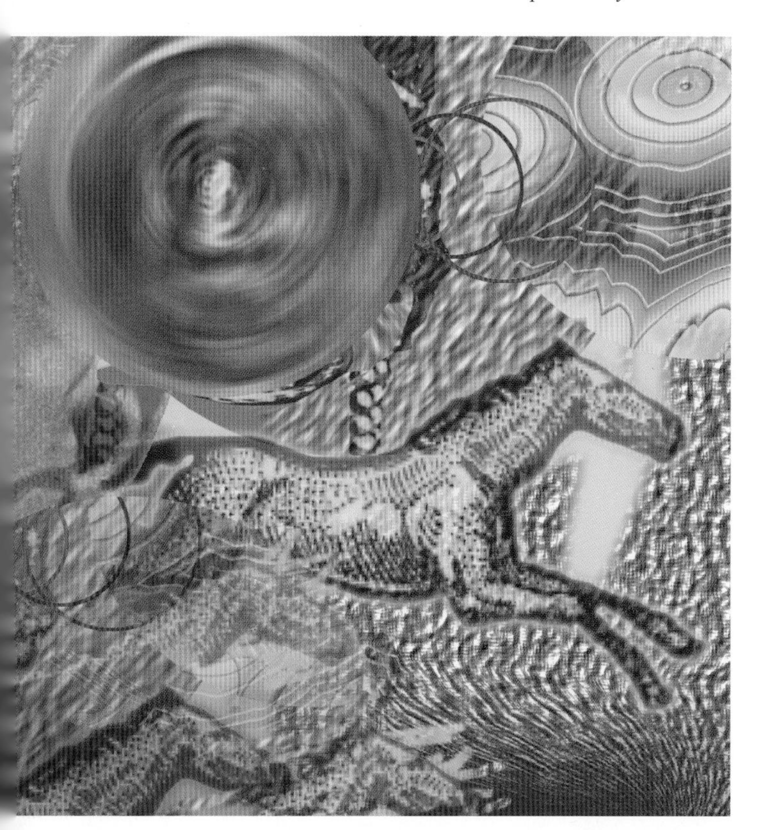

Dream symbols
You may need to think laterally when trying to interpret images and pictures in your dreams

It does this because your unconscious wants to bring to the forefront of your mind the expression "a chip off the old block." Yesterday, as you stood at the kitchen window watching your son, something in his movements reminded you of his father. At the time, it was a fleeting impression, a half-conscious thought. But now your sleeping mind has time to pick up on that theme and to develop the half-thought to its full implications. It does this ingeniously and economically by combining the event you were witnessing with the thoughts you had at the time. In this way, your dream uses the chipped wood to point out that your son is like his father.

MOVING UP A LEVEL

But why leave it there when there is so much more to say? By going up yet another level of meaning and analyzing the symbolism, it is even possible to tell something about your state of mind – how you feel at the moment and how your life is going. The predominant feeling in the dream is that of warmth and coziness. Fire symbolizes warmth and passions. Here the fire is burning nicely, so you have your feelings well in control, and you are contented and untroubled. There are more logs waiting to go on the fire, which suggests that the contentment will last.

Furthermore, eating in our dreams symbolizes nurturing of a physical, emotional, intellectual or spiritual kind. The fact that you are eating together implies that you are a united family, supportive of each other. It is, then, a most reassuring dream, which reflects feelings of satisfaction and a strong sense of fulfillment in your current situation and domestic way of life.

RHYTHMS OF SLEEP

Whether you are an insomniac or the sort of person who goes out like a light the minute your head touches the pillow, once you have dropped off, research shows that your sleep will follow a set pattern. For the first ten minutes you will drift in a twilight world, held beween consciousness and unconsciousness. Slowly, you begin to sink deeper and deeper, until you are at your most relaxed, and as far away from wakefulness as sleeping will allow.

Reaching this stage of deep sleep takes roughly forty-five minutes, after which you begin to reverse the journey, climbing up again to the top levels of lighter sleep. In all, the sinking and rising form a wave pattern that takes some ninety minutes to complete and which then repeats itself over and over again, sometimes four, five, even six times throughout the night, depending on the duration of sleep.

Specific physical changes accompany the sleep cycle. In deep sleep, brain activity is reduced, blood pressure drops, and our breathing slows down. At this stage we lose muscle tone, our limbs are heavy, and our bodies are in a state similar to paralysis. Chemical changes also take place now. Growth hormone, secreted from the pituitary gland, enables the body to grow and the tissues to repair themselves.

But it is during the lighter phases of sleep that most of our dreaming takes place. As we rise out of deep sleep, blood-flow to the brain begins to increase, as does brain activity. At this point, both our breathing and pulse rates become erratic and blood pressure begins to rise. Our eyes begin to move around beneath our closed eyelids as if we were watching a film on a screen, and it is this, known as rapid eye movement, or REM, that shows we are dreaming. Our muscles are still deeply relaxed, presumably to disable us from acting out our dreams.

Wave pattern
Deep and lighter sleep phases alternate, like ocean waves, throughout the night

fascinating facts about sleep

- In an average lifetime we spend in the region of twenty-five years asleep.
- Old wives' tales that encourage us to get our beauty sleep are not far off the mark, since it is while we sleep that our bodies heal and repair themselves.
- The amount of sleep each person needs varies with the individual. The average requirement is around six or seven hours, although some people cannot cope with fewer than ten.
- The duration of sleep we require also varies at different times in our lives. Babies sleep almost continuously through the day and night. However, adults need less and less sleep as they get older. Elderly people sleep least of all.

WHY DO WE DREAM?

Despite the wealth of scientific investigation that has taken place over the last century into the analysis of dreaming and the processes of sleeping, researchers in this field are still no nearer to understanding precisely why it is we dream. We know exactly when in the sleep cycle we dream, we know how long our dreams last, we know who tends to dream more about certain types of subjects, and we can itemize what we dream about. But, although many theories have been put forward, the truth of the matter is we simply don't know why we dream.

Sleep therapy
Dreams can help us cope with life in the waking world

Certainly, researchers have discovered that dreaming is essential to our well-being because we suffer physically if we are deprived of the opportunity to dream. Equally, although not everyone agrees on all the reasons, the general consensus is that we derive enormous benefit from our dreams.

Experiments have been carried out to explore the effects of dream deprivation. Researchers have found that our ability to concentrate on a task or on our work is impaired, and that we tend to daydream more. If dream deprivation continues for too long, we may even suffer hallucinations. Emotionally, we may become unstable, experiencing erratic or irrational moods and feelings. It is also interesting to find that if, for whatever reason, we are denied our chance to dream, we make up for this lack as soon as we can by cramming in more dreaming time the very next opportunity we get to sleep.

The benefits of dreaming are nevertheless acknowledged. It is believed that dreams somehow help us evaluate the events of the day by sorting and sifting, cataloging and imprinting, and finally dumping or storing these images in our memory banks. Our

Images of fear

Even nightmares can help us find solutions to our problems

dreams, it is believed, offer our minds a break from the pressures of the day. They provide an overview of our experiences, allow us to reassess events that have taken place, or link us with the past by reviewing memories and past experiences that we have undergone. Moreover, it is in our dreams that we can sort through our personal problems and examine inhibitions because, in showing us the unvarnished truth about ourselves, they help us to face up to the realities of our waking lives.

If we learn how to interpret our dreams, we will gain self-knowledge and crystal-clear insights about our relationships, our motivations, and our development and direction in life. But there is even more to gain, because, by synthesizing information that was only partially observed or processed by our conscious, waking minds, our dreams can give us advance warnings, or prepare us for stressful events. And, like the best friends that we could ever wish to have, our dreams can commiserate with us when we feel blue, and even pat us on the back when we need to be congratulated.

Dreams come in all shapes, colors and sizes, and we don't remember all of them. Far from it – in fact, it has been estimated that we forget about 95 percent of them. Those that we do recall are the most vivid ones, and because of that, these are the dreams we consider to be important and worthy of interpreting.

fascinating facts about dreaming

- Researchers in dream laboratories have observed that when we dream our eyeballs roll around beneath our closed eyelids just as if we were "watching" a movie. They have termed this phenomenon REM, which stands for rapid eye movement. The periods in our sleep when we dream are therefore known as REM sleep, as opposed to those times when we don't dream, which are called NREM, or non-REM, sleep.
- By using ultrasound scans, scientists have discovered that prenatal babies experience REM sleep as early as in the sixth month of their development. This suggests that even babies in the womb dream.
- Over half the amount of time a newborn baby spends asleep is taken up by dreaming. A one-year-old baby will dream for up to five hours each night.
- An adult dreams for up to two hours during a good night's rest, but dream time lessens as people get older.
- In an average lifetime, an individual may spend around ten years of his or her life dreaming.

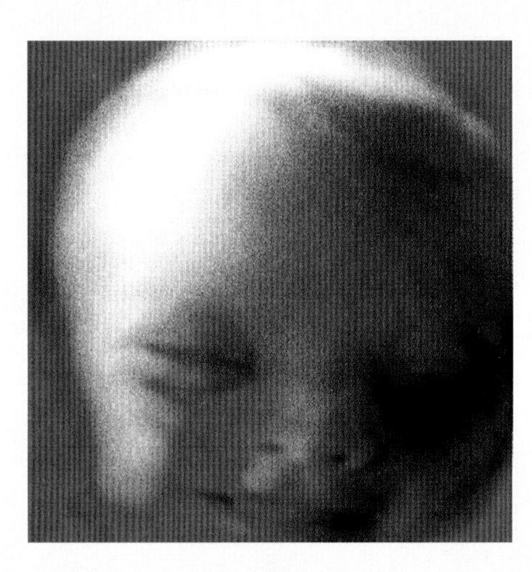

- The duration of dreams varies. Some last for five minutes, while others can take one hour to unfold. Shorter dreams occur at the beginning of sleep and gradually lengthen through the night. The longest dreams are usually experienced before waking up in the morning.
- The visual images, flashes of light, or distorted pictures that we sometimes see just as we fall asleep are called hypnogogic visions. They are a halfway stage between consciousness and unconsciousness, and as such are not classified as proper dreams.
- Although events may be condensed, or incidents from different historical eras brought together, dreams occur in real time, which means that they actually last for as long as it takes the drama to "play itself through."
- According to dream scientists, we forget as many as 95 percent of our dreams. Everyone dreams, but people who say they never do simply cannot remember their dreams. We are more likely to recall a dream if we wake up during or just after REM sleep. Waking up at any other stage in the sleep cycle reduces our chances of remembering our dreams.
- When we dream, important chemical changes take place in the brain. Levels of the fight-flight hormone, noradrenaline, and serotonin, the mood controller, are lowered whilst acetylcholine, which activates the brain, is increased.
- Alcohol, sleeping pills, and other drugs can inhibit our ability to dream.
- Physical discomfort, such as going to sleep on a full stomach, or being too hot in bed, can trigger nightmares. Medical conditions such as feverishness or indigestion can also cause bad dreams.

- Most mammals show evidence of REM sleep, and research suggests that animals dream, too – a fact that most owners of cats and dogs would confirm from observing the spasms of twitching whiskers and limbs of their sleeping pets.
- Although greatly reduced, we still have an awareness of environmental stimuli such as noises or smells that take place around us while we sleep. Direct evidence of this can be seen in the dreams in which we weave the ring of an alarm clock, or the mailman's knock, into the action of a dream. For example, the sound of a neighbor mowing the lawn might be incorporated into a dream story about a drive in a car.

DREAMING THROUGH HISTORY

Exactly when people began to take notice of their dreams is unknown, but evidence in clay tablets dating from around 5,000 B.C.E. exists, proving that men and women were already fascinated by the meaning of their dreams. Interestingly, even in those days the Babylonians and Assyrians found a sexual element in dream imagery, foreshadowing Freud's theories by thousands of years. Dreams about flying, too, appear to have been as common at that time as they are to us now. People of the ancient world took their dreams seriously, believing them to be messages from the gods – both of good and evil. They also put great store in the predictive aspects of dreaming, and developed techniques for inducing, or "incubating," dreams precisely so that they might see their destinies and anticipate future events. The Bible, for example, is liberally sprinkled with stories of prophetic dreams and visions, Joseph's interpretation of the Pharoah's dream being one of the most famous examples ever recorded. It was Joseph's correct interpretation of this dream, which warned of a catastrophic crop failure, and the Pharoah's judicious response – to stockpile grain – that saved Egypt from the devastating effects of widespread famine.

For thousands of years the cultures of indigenous tribes, ranging from the Native Americans, to the Ashanti people of West Africa, to the Aborigines of Australia, have been rich in dream traditions and dream lore. The Sioux and the Iroquois, for example, held dream festivals in which they would dance and reenact their dreams. The Ashanti believed that their ancestors spoke to them in their dreams. But no more important can the concept of dreaming be than to the Aborigines, whose belief that the universe was created in the Dreamtime is fundamental to their traditions and way of life.

Eastern philosophers, ever adept at probing the depths of the human psyche, were far advanced in the understanding of dreams and their meanings long ago. Writings dating back to around 500 B.C.E. show that the Chinese, for example, acknowledged various categories of dreams and were aware of different levels of dream interpretation. From India, too, historians have discovered evidence that shows a recognition of the different stages of sleep some three millennia before dream researchers in the west established REM and other phases of sleep through scientific methods.

Literary dreams

The biblical tales about Joseph show that dreams have had symbolic significance for thousands of years

The great thinkers of the Greco-Roman world, among them Hippocrates and Plato, were also interested in the subject of dreams. Hippocrates saw a therapeutic, or cathartic, function in dreams, while Plato reasoned that it is in our dreams that our emotions are allowed free rein.

It was in the second century C.E. that Artemidorus, a major figure in the history of dream research, gathered together a vast collection of writings and dream examples from which he formulated his theories on the meanings of dreams. He was one of the first to state that dreams had to be understood in context, and that the dreamer's personality and circumstances in life had to be taken into consideration in order to arrive at a clear interpretation. He set down these ideas in what was to become the most influential book on this subject of its time. Despite the intervening years, the ideas promulgated by Artemidorus are, in many ways, forerunners of our own modern thinking on the nature of dreaming, and have led directly to the psychoanalytical approach adopted by more recent dream scientists.

THE DREAM ANALYSTS

The development of psychoanalysis in modern times has been the major influence in the understanding of dreams. Among the early pioneers, three names stand head and shoulders above the rest – Freud, Jung, and Adler. Freud, father of the analytical technique, was the prime innovator; Jung brought insight and depth of vision; and Adler saw the therapeutic potential of dreams. Collectively, these three not only advanced our understanding of the psyche, but also irrevocably changed the way in which we think about and interpret our dreams.

SIGMUND FREUD

1856–1939

Born in Austria, Freud began his career as a doctor and specialized in the treatment of mental disorders. He coined the term "psychoanalysis" and developed techniques for exploring the unconscious mind, which involved analyzing his patients' dreams. He believed that dreams reveal the workings of our waking minds, and saw parallels between conscious behavior and the symbolic imagery of dreams. Coming as he did from an age of sexual repression when such matters were never openly discussed, he perhaps overemphasized the covertly erotic creations of the unconscious mind, interpreting a great many dream symbols as projections of inhibited passions or suppressed desires. He encouraged his patients to talk through their dreams, and pioneered the technique of "free association," whereby a key word or concept would spark an associated event or emotion, and thereby give vital clues to the meaning of the dream.

The unconscious mind
The work of analysts such as Carl Jung heralded greater interest in dream interpretation

CARL GUSTAV JUNG

1875–1961

A contemporary of Freud, although nineteen years his junior, Jung is best known for formulating the theory of the "collective

unconscious." This he described as a reservoir of racial memories and experiences that we all share and to which we all have access. This pool contains what he termed "archetypes" – the basic ideas or concepts that, regardless of race, sex, language, or creed, will nevertheless be understood in exactly the same way by everyone, because each archetype conveys a universal truth that applies equally to every human being.

Archetypes, Jung argued, are passed down to us through the generations from our early ancestors. It is through our dreams that we are able to "dip" into this communal fund, just as we might access information on the Internet, and pick up symbols which, although of universal signficance, aptly represent the very situation that our own subconscious minds want to bring to our attention.

ALFRED ADLER

1870–1937

Adler had much in common with Freud. Both men were born in Austria in the second half of the nineteenth century, studying medicine and collaborating with each other before working in the field of psychiatry with mentally ill patients. It was Adler, though, who went on to develop the theory that individuals are strongly affected by their personal sense of power – or lack of it – and coined the terms "superiority complex" and "inferiority complex" to describe this effect. He believed that by understanding our dreams we can recognize and work through these complexes. Unlike Freud, Adler maintained that dream experiences and emotions could be carried over into our waking lives and used to heal our problems.

Therapeutic images

For Freud, a single image could provide the key to a dream

DREAM THEMES

Since dream laboratories were first set up in the 1950s, researchers have gathered a great deal of information not only about the types of dreams that we experience, but also about their subject matter and contents. Men's dreams, it appears, differ significantly from those of women, and children's dreams are different still. Moreover, it has also been found that, regardless of age or sex, certain subjects tend to emerge more often than others.

VIVE LA DIFFÉRENCE

Scientists have discovered that even in dreams the sexes focus on different interests and aspects of life. By interviewing thousands of people about their dreams, a pattern regarding those differences has emerged.

- In general, women tend to be more verbally expressive when it comes to relating their dreams to others, and have fewer inhibitions about disclosing the contents of their dreams. Men, however, perhaps because dreaming is seen as "emotional," either get embarrassed or tend not to be so forthcoming when asked to discuss their nighttime reveries.
- Men's dreams are populated more by male figures than female ones. Similarly, women dream more about other women than they do about men.
- People, relationships, houses, furniture, clothes, and jewelry appear more frequently in women's dreams, while action, adventures, cars, sports, machinery, and tools feature more often in the dreams of men.
- When it comes to erotic dreams, men tend to dream about the physical aspects of sex, but women's dreams have a more romantic slant rather than focusing on the physical act.
- In sexual dreams, women more often than not can put either a name or a face to the person they are with. Men, on the other hand, have admitted that they do not always recognize their dream partner.
- As a comment on dreaming in general, men dislike the feeling of not being in control of the action, a factor that does not disturb women dreamers to the same extent.

common dream themes

Water · Being trapped · Travel · Running · Being chased · Death · Falling · Houses and buildings · Flying · Nudity · Being late · Sex

CHILDREN'S DREAMS

Because children sleep for longer, they naturally have more dreams than adults do. Although it is difficult to know what very young infants, let alone prenatal babies, might dream about, older children report that they tend to dream a good deal about animals. Many dreams that children experience are frightening, containing monsters, wild beasts, and bogeymen of all descriptions. As many parents are all too uncomfortably aware, children are prone to nightmares, waking up in the middle of the night either in terror or in tears. For many, these bad dreams have a habit of recurring and only disappear when the fears and anxieties of their waking lives are either understood, or a solution found. But interestingly, too, youngsters experience predictive or precognitive dreams as a matter of course, without any of the consternation about this type of dream that often affects their elders.

Sweet dreams

As they come to understand the world around them, children grow out of nightmares

A ROLE FOR EVERY DREAM

We know that our dreams are important to our well-being because it has been proven that dream-deprivation causes physical and mental after-effects. And although we may not be entirely sure, we do believe that in some way our dreams help us to make sense of events that occur in the day. This seems to be borne out by the variety of dreams that we experience: some appear to act as simple recordings of what has taken place, while others are loaded with symbolism, drawing our attention to things that are going on "behind the scenes," or at the peripheries of our conscious awareness.

Some dreams, it appears, are warnings, and some act as reminders. Some bring facts to our attention, while others help us to resolve our problems. Some are creative and others are frightening; there are those that make us laugh and others that take the sting out of the harsh realities of our waking lives.

With such diversity, we can only conclude that our dreams play different roles for us at different times in our lives, and we cannot but accept that they unfold themselves to us according to our needs.

Looking back
Our dreams may review the events of the day and the people we met

FACTUAL DREAMS

Since we only remember five percent of our dreams, this must indicate that not all of our nighttime reveries are so full of meaning that we must be made consciously aware of their messages. Perhaps the majority of our dreams perform a simple, basic function, but one that is nevertheless extremely important in order to keep the working surfaces of our minds clear and ready for another day. These we may call factual dreams, which register, sift, sort, and generally tidy up the experiences of our waking hours.

INSIGHT DREAMS

These dreams piece together the suspicions or intuitive glimpses that come to us in our waking lives. They allow us to make sudden discoveries, either to see the unvarnished truth about a situation or to reveal our true feelings about a person. In short, insight dreams confirm our misgivings and bring to our attention those things that we may have refused to look at or to accept.

REMINDER DREAMS

Reminder dreams are handy memos. They jog our memories or pick up on unfinished business from our waking hours. Prompting us to take back library books, reminding us to keep a dental appointment, or bringing to mind a relative's birthday, are all within the remit of this type of dream.

WISH-FULFILLMENT DREAMS

In these dreams we redress the balance of our waking lives. Here the impecunious win the lottery, those on a diet enjoy a banquet, and unhappy lovers are reunited. Wish-fulfillment dreams are literally "the stuff that dreams are made on."

PRECOGNITIVE DREAMS

Also known as predictive dreams, these give us foreknowledge and either alert us to opportunites or give us advance warnings of situations to come. Whether they are based on intuitive guesses or come completely out of the blue is still a matter for conjecture. Many people, however, claim to have foreseen disasters such as the sinking of the Titanic or the eruption of Krakatoa weeks before the events took place.

ANXIETY DREAMS

This category of dreams includes feelings of embarrassment, abandonment, fear of ridicule or failure, or any other situation that brings to the forefront of our minds the worries we have when we are awake.

Caught in a trap
Nightmares may reflect our personal fears and anxieties

NIGHTMARES

Sometimes these are triggered by physiological causes such as a feverish condition or an over-full stomach. Otherwise, and more seriously, these dreams may be caused by deep-seated, traumatic problems in our waking lives, and bring to our attention fears that must be resolved. Only when we address and find a solution to our problems will these nightmares disappear.

EROTIC DREAMS

Of course, no discussion about erotic dreams would be complete without acknowledging the immense contribution Freud made to this subject, with his pioneering work on the sexual symbolism of dreams. However, recent studies have shown that incidents of dream eroticism are far fewer than Freudians would have us believe, ranking well down the list of common dream themes. In fact, some dream analysts say that less than one percent of our dreams have anything to do with sex.

RELEASE OF TENSION

Dreams involving sexual acts may be a simple mechanism to give our minds and bodies a means of releasing tension. Indeed, researchers tell us that penile erection is a common occurrence during dreaming, and it is not unusual to experience an orgasm in our sleep. Since love is fundamental to our psychological well-being and procreation is essential to ensure the continuity of our species, dreams featuring these aspects of our lives can only be seen as natural and healthy – the bonus is that they can be very enjoyable into the bargain. Of course, some erotic dreams are simply wish-fulfillment. Sexual fantasies in our waking lives or a longing to be reunited with a lost lover, for example, can innocently be satisfied in our dreams.

Dark secrets
Sexual repression in Freud's era led to his concentration on sexual symbolism in dreams

PERSONALITY POINTERS

We need not automatically read unconscious sexual motivation into all dreams that contain the slightest hint of explicit eroticism, as many of them may not so much point out repressed desire, but, may comment on aspects of our personality instead. For a woman to dream that she has a penis, for example, need not imply latent lesbian tendencies, but a symbolic recognition of her strengths – her assertiveness, courage, or logical mentality, qualities that we consider to be masculine. Similarly, a man dreaming that he has breasts may be his way of acknowledging his feminine characteristics – the fact that his nature is caring, nurturing or intuitive, perhaps.

SEXUAL IMAGERY

Much Freudian dream interpretation centers around phallic symbols. Anything long or penile in shape, such as a tower, a snake, a gun, or a knife, for example, would be immediately pounced upon as a representation of the male sexual organ. Similarly, containers or any other object that can be entered, such as a bag or purse, or even shoes, would be thought of as representing the female sexual organs, the vagina and uterus. Certainly, while we may associate long, thin objects with penises, and containers with the womb, we should not lose sight of the alternative levels of interpretation that our subconscious minds may be working on. So a candle, for example, rather than symbolizing a penis, may be representing light, hope, insight, or enlightenment, and the object it illuminates may provide answers to problems. Entering a dark cave, so often suggested as a desire to "go back to the womb," or as symbolic of sexual penetration, may be reflecting waking anxieties about an uncertain future, like, for example, the fears of a person suddenly made redundant.

Simple pleasures
Erotic dreams can often provide a harmless and healthy way of releasing sexual tension

LUCID DREAMS

A special type of dream has been attracting interest over the last twenty years in particular. These are called lucid dreams. They are fascinating not only because they differ significantly from other types of dreams, but also because a different kind of awareness comes into play here. The actual term "lucid" implies a clarity of vision, an ability to see through the dream and to recognize that we are actually dreaming. It is precisely this higher state of awareness within the dream that puts lucid dreaming into a category of its own.

ALTERED STATES OF CONSCIOUSNESS

In conventional dreams, reality is distorted: heads may be disproportionately bigger than the bodies they are on, cars drive unscathed through brick walls, the grass is purple, and pigs can fly. As dreamers, we take all this in our stride. We walk on water, talk to long-dead relatives, and grow necks as long as those belonging to the giraffes that roam the Serengeti plains. We accept the impossible. Events that, in our waking hours we would instantly dismiss as absurd and illogical, appear in our dreams as rational, feasible, and unquestionably possible.

It is not so in lucid dreams. In lucid dreams, a higher level of awareness takes over – we recognize irrational events for what they are, and we can spot discrepancies between dream events and those that take place in our everyday lives. In lucid dreams, if something isn't quite right, we instantly become suspicious. It is this very recognition that tells us we are experiencing a lucid dream. Though we are still fast asleep, we suddenly know that we are dreaming, and this realization acts like a trigger. Indeed, some dream researchers have called this moment "the lightbulb effect."

A DREAM INSIDE A DREAM

At this point in the dream, we are given the opportunity to take control of the action. If we choose, we can switch into a different mode: now we can call the shots. It's like a play within a play and we can, at the very same time, direct the action as well as star in the production, too. Taking control of the action in this way effectively means that we are in dialog with our unconscious and we can knowingly access any part of the information stored there. Instead of our unconscious offering up information to us, we choose which pieces of information we wish to resource. This gives us a golden opportunity to sort out any problems that are troubling our waking lives, to increase our creative aware-

ness, or to find inventive solutions to matters that are puzzling us. Through lucid dreaming, and this direct contact with our unconscious, we can explore our hidden motivations and drives, seek out the source of our anxieties, and find a way of coming to terms with them. Lucid dreams are thus of immense value.

EXHILARATING IMAGES

We are more likely to experience lucid dreams early in the morning or when we take light naps rather than during a heavy sleep. In lucid dreams, images and colors are much more intense than usual, and experiencing them leaves us exhilarated.

A flash of excitement
Lucid dreams often involve exhilarating experiences

INSPIRATIONAL AND PRECOGNITIVE DREAMS

Dreams have been, and continue to be, a source of creative inspiration to more inventive minds than many people might care to admit. Our history is peppered with scientific discoveries, inspirational political thought, and literary and musical masterpieces that have been helped along by the spark of genius generated by the sleeping mind. The opportunity to catch glimpses of the future are also offered to us, whether or not we choose to act on the information we receive. How, one wonders, might the fortunes of the Roman Empire, let alone the course of history, have been changed had Julius Caesar heeded his wife's forebodings? For Calpurnia, it has been said, dreamt of her husband's assassination several days before his death, but, unfortunately, Caesar failed to take her warnings seriously.

Creative inspiration
Many artists and thinkers have found inspiration in their dreams

INVENTORS AND SCIENTISTS

Einstein, arguably one of the greatest geniuses of our time, admitted that the idea that led to the Theory of Relativity came to him in a dream when he was a young man.

It was a dream about a Native American jabbing a spear in the air, an eye-hole in its tip, that gave the inventor Elias Howe the idea to design a sewing machine.

Thanks to a dream about a snake with its tail in its mouth, Friedrich Kekulé, a German chemist, was able to figure out the structure of the benzene molecule.

MUSICIANS

Many musicians have claimed to have heard music playing in their dreams which they later integrated into their compositions. The Italian composer Giuseppe Tartini is one such example. A dream also inspired Wagner to write the music for *Tristan and Isolde*. And in more modern times, Paul McCartney has revealed that he dreamed the tune for

"Yesterday", which has become not only one of the most famous, but also one of the most frequently played songs ever written.

WRITERS AND ARTISTS

It was in a dream that the poem *Kubla Khan* came to Samuel Taylor Coleridge, who, immediately on waking, began furiously writing it down. Unfortunately, he was disturbed by a visitor before he could finish and the rest of the vision was driven from his mind, never to return.

Robert Louis Stevenson has described how he dreamt a dramatic scene that sowed the germ of an idea into his memory, which he then developed into the story of *Dr. Jekyll and Mr. Hyde.*

The author Graham Greene has recounted how, by rereading his work before going to sleep, his unconscious mind would then take over and, on waking, he would find ready insights into his characters, and the plot would simply follow on. Greene also told how, as a child, he foresaw in a dream the disaster of the Titanic only a few nights before it sank.

Both the painter Albrecht Dürer and the visionary poet and illustrator William Blake have attributed paintings and other pieces of their work to their dreams.

The poet Percy Bysshe Shelley foresaw his own death and that of his friend a few weeks before they drowned together in a sailing accident off the coast of Italy.

POLITICAL FIGURES

English revolutionary leader Oliver Cromwell dreamt that one day he would come to rule the whole of England, a fact revealed to him by a female figure. At the time, when the royal succession to the throne was an unassailable fact, such a prediction must have seemed impossible. Perhaps it was this dream, however, that provided the spur which gave Cromwell the confidence to overthrow King Charles I and take the title of Lord Protector in 1653.

As a young man, Adolf Hitler saved his own life by heeding a premonition he had in a dream. He jumped out of a trench in the First World War minutes before it was devastated by a bomb.

Abraham Lincoln dreamt about his death some days before his assassination by the actor and Confederate sympathizer John Wilkes Booth.

Dire warnings
The artist's unconscious can be a source of forebodings as well as creativity

HOW TO RECALL YOUR DREAMS

Obvious though it might seem, in order to remember your dream, you must first have a dream, which means getting a good night's rest. But, as importantly as having that restful sleep, you must wake up at the right moment in your sleep cycle to enable you to recall the dream. Waking up during, or just after REM sleep is ideal, but sleeping on into a different part of the cycle will make the process of remembering a dream that much more difficult, if not impossible.

BEFORE YOU FALL ASLEEP

First, read the sleep-aiding tips on the facing page, then check that you have your dream journal and a pencil by your bedside. As you lie in bed, make sure you are warm and comfortable and settle into your favorite "sleep position." Now think about what is preoccupying you most at this moment in your waking life. It might be a worry about someone you love, frustrations at work, a need to solve a problem, a lack of inspiration, loneliness, or a challenge. Form those concerns clearly in your mind and frame them into a simple question: "What do I do about such-and-such?," or "Where do I go from here?," or "Which one should I choose?"

Some people find that actually writing the question down can help to crystallize and focus it in their minds. Perhaps you could write the question in your dream journal and when you wake up you can add the dream beneath it. This technique is also useful as it helps to set the scene, or describe what is

Dreamtime
In order to enter fully into your dreamworld, you need to ensure a peaceful night's sleep

happening in your waking life. Your subsequent dream will then comment upon the situation you have described.

Once you have your question clearly in mind, ask your unconscious to deal with it, to give you direction, guidance, insight, fresh inspiration, or whatever you require. Now, try a bit of auto-suggestion. Tell yourself that you will remember your dream. Go over the question in your mind and reaffirm to yourself that you will remember your dream. Repeat this affirmation as you physically relax. Feel your limbs getting heavier and heavier, your body sinking deeper and deeper into the bed, and your mind drifting, drifting, drifting slowly away.

tips to ensure a good night's rest

Do

- have a warm, relaxing bath before bed
- drink a cup of chamomile or other herbal tea
- read a book or listen to soothing music
- try a few deep-breathing relaxation exercises
- practice meditation
- ask your partner to give you a soothing massage

Don't

- drink coffee in the evening
- take catnaps in the daytime
- eat a heavy meal just before bed
- lie in bed if you can't sleep – get up, find something calming to do for 15 minutes and then try again
- go to bed hungry – low blood glucose levels can keep you awake

RECORDING YOUR DREAMS

Wake up slowly – leaping out of bed is likely to drive the dream clean out of your mind. Lie still with your eyes closed and "relive" the dream. Now write it down. Don't leave it until later because you are likely to forget the intricacies. It is important that you should write down as much detail – images, symbols, color, moods, and impressions – as you can. Note any people or places you recognized, whether something didn't quite match with a person or a situation you know in waking life. If not, ask yourself why not? What was significant about those discrepancies? When was the dream set – recently, some years ago or perhaps at some time in the future? What type of dream was it – happy, sad, or embarrassing? Was it a nightmare, or perhaps a wish-fulfillment or problem-solving dream?

Instant recall
Like a child telling a story, you need to write down your dreams as soon as you wake, or you risk forgetting details

It is of great importance that you make a note of the emotions you felt, not only throughout the dream, but also when it was over and you woke up. You will find that the emotions you experienced will hold the key to the meaning of the dream.

KEEPING A DREAM JOURNAL WILL:

- make it easier to interpret your dreams
- illustrate the evolution, changes, and developments of recurring dreams
- clarify the problems and anxieties of your waking life
- help you to gain insights about yourself and others
- enable you to see patterns of behavior, issues, and emotions that govern your life
- bring to light your deepest thoughts, hidden desires, and heartfelt wishes
- offer self-awareness and give you a clearer understanding of your drives and motivations in life

AND FINALLY

Fitful sleep inhibits dreaming: check that you have no underlying health problems that affect your sleep. If you find it difficult to remember your dreams, examine your diet – drugs, alcohol, or a deficiency of vitamin B6 may inhibit dreaming.

Last, but not least, if you wake up halfway through a dream, or if the dream has been disturbing, lie still and try to reenter the action. Go through it again in your mind and give it a more satisfactory ending. This is a valuable visualization technique that can help give you the confidence to resolve any difficulties you may be experiencing in your waking life.

part two

AIDS TO RESTFUL SLEEP AND PEACEFUL DREAMING

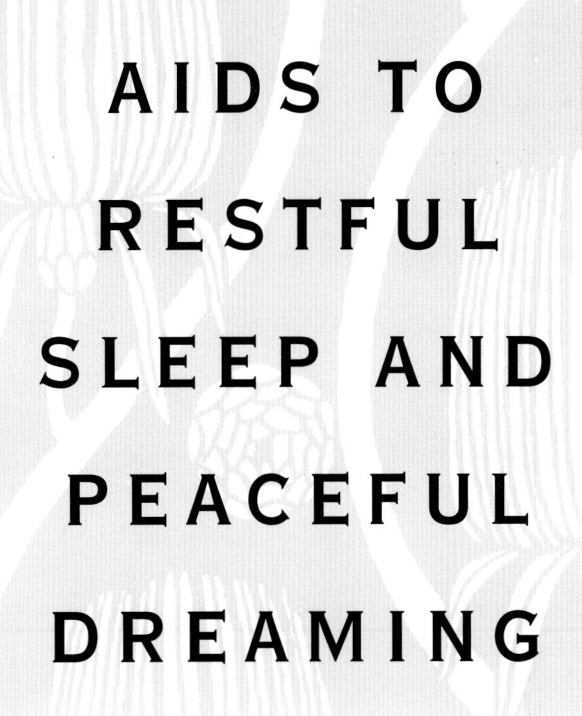

THE DREAM CATCHER

Originally made by the Native Americans, dream catchers are now often given as gifts to friends and lovers, to mark the union of two people, or in celebration of the birth of a baby. According to legend, bad dreams are caught in the web and dissolve away at dawn.

Consisting of a ring surrounding a web, and adorned with beads and feathers, the dream catcher is hung at a window, by the door or above a cot to act as a filter of dreams. Good dreams permeate through the centre of the web, and are either dreamed just once or stored in the decorations to be dreamed anew another time. The examples shown here may be appropriate for particular people or particular occasions. Make your own dream web and weave it with love to ensure that sweet dreams will always fill your sleeping hours.

You will need

An 8in (20cm) diameter wooden ring (available from craft stores)

7ft (2m) 3-ply embroidery thread

A needle (thin enough to go through the beads but with a wide eye)

8 beads

For decoration

Shells, glass or wooden beads, feathers, ribbons, small wooden toys, bows, lace, satin roses, leather tassels, dried leaves, silk flowers, etc.

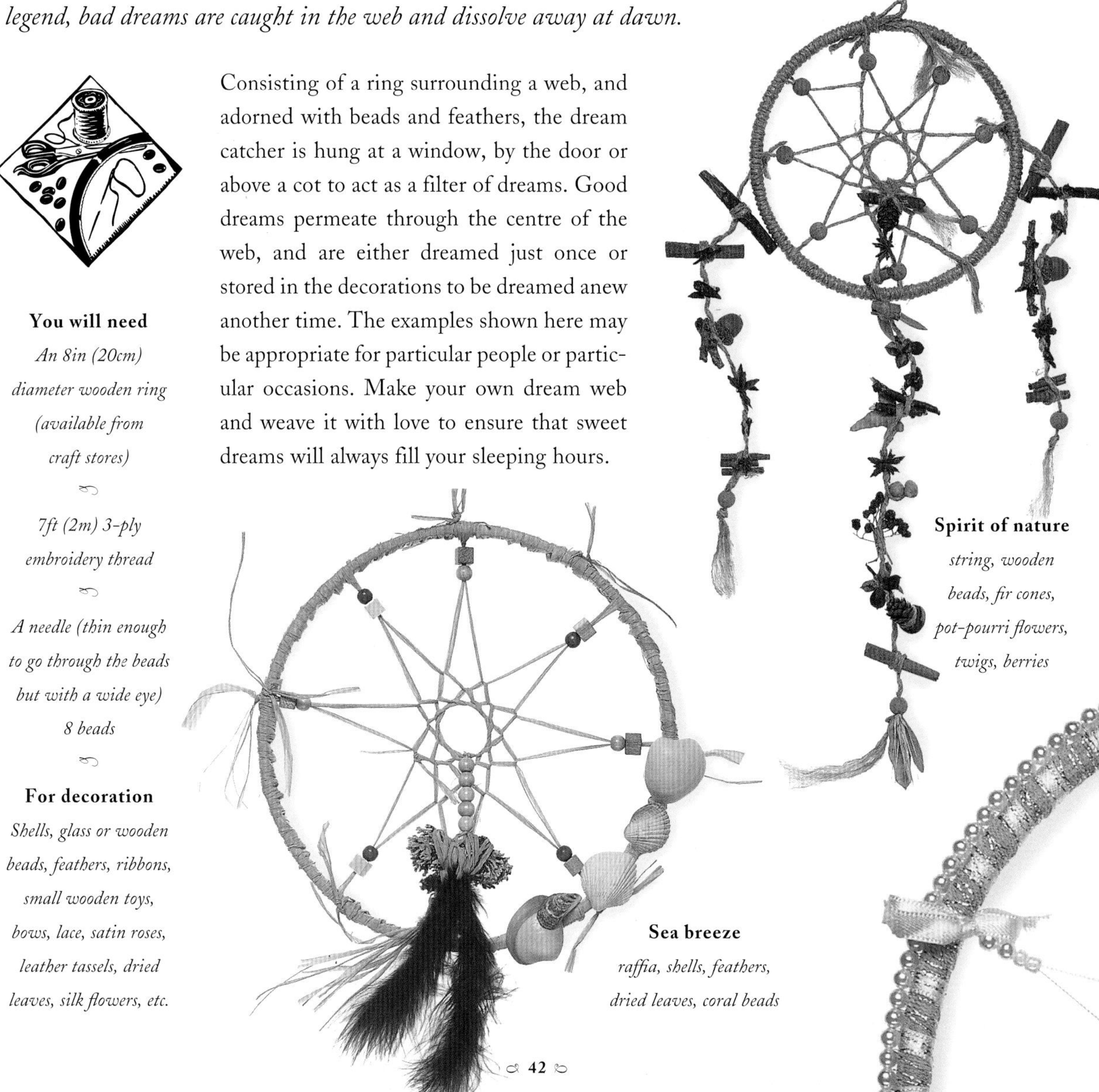

Spirit of nature

string, wooden beads, fir cones, pot-pourri flowers, twigs, berries

Sea breeze

raffia, shells, feathers, dried leaves, coral beads

instructions to make a dream catcher

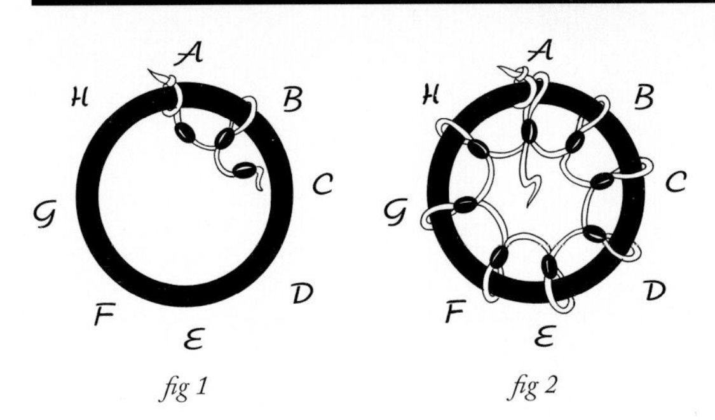

fig 1 *fig 2*

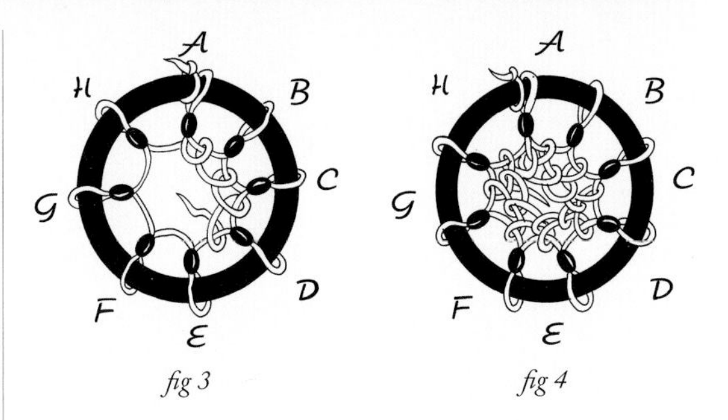

fig 3 *fig 4*

FIGURE 1

- *Divide the ring into 8 equal sections from A to H and mark with a pencil. Thread the needle and tie securely around point A to anchor. Pull thread tight and thread on 2 beads.*
- *Loop thread in clockwise direction around point B and pass the thread back through the second bead as in the diagram.*
- *Keeping the thread tight at all times, thread on a third bead and loop clockwise around point C. Bring the thread back through the third bead and work towards the next point.*
- *Work around the ring in this way, threading through each bead, until point H is reached.*

FIGURE 2

- *At point H, wind the thread clockwise around the ring and then back through the eighth bead. Now insert the thread through the first bead and up to point A. Wind the thread clockwise around point A and back through the first bead again.*

FIGURE 3

- *Bring the thread up and over the first loop between the first and second beads. Continue in this way around the web, winding the thread up and through the centre of each loop until the mid-point of H and A is reached and an inner ring of loops has been made.*
- *From this point pass the thread up and through the new loop between A and B, then through the second loop at B and C, and so on in a spiral formation, making ever-decreasing circles until the ring is filled with a cobweb of intertwined loops.*

FIGURE 4

- *When the ring is complete, a tiny, perfect circle will be formed at the centre. At this point, pass the thread through and tie a knot to secure, but do not cut off this end. Leave a 12 in. (30cm) length of thread on which to thread beads, pearls, feathers, shells, etc., to form a tassel.*

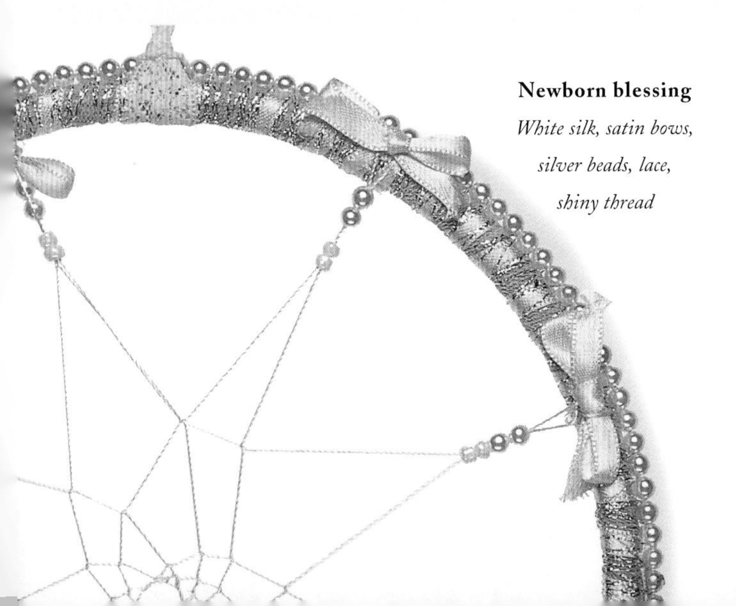

Newborn blessing

White silk, satin bows, silver beads, lace, shiny thread

Presents

A hand-made dream catcher is a sign of your affection for a friend or lover

HERBS FOR HEALTHY SLEEP

"Lettuce," wrote Nicholas Culpeper, the great seventeenth-century English physician and herbalist, "gently disposes the patient to sleep." In further extoling the virtues of this herb, he tells us that it also has the power to "repress venereous dreams."

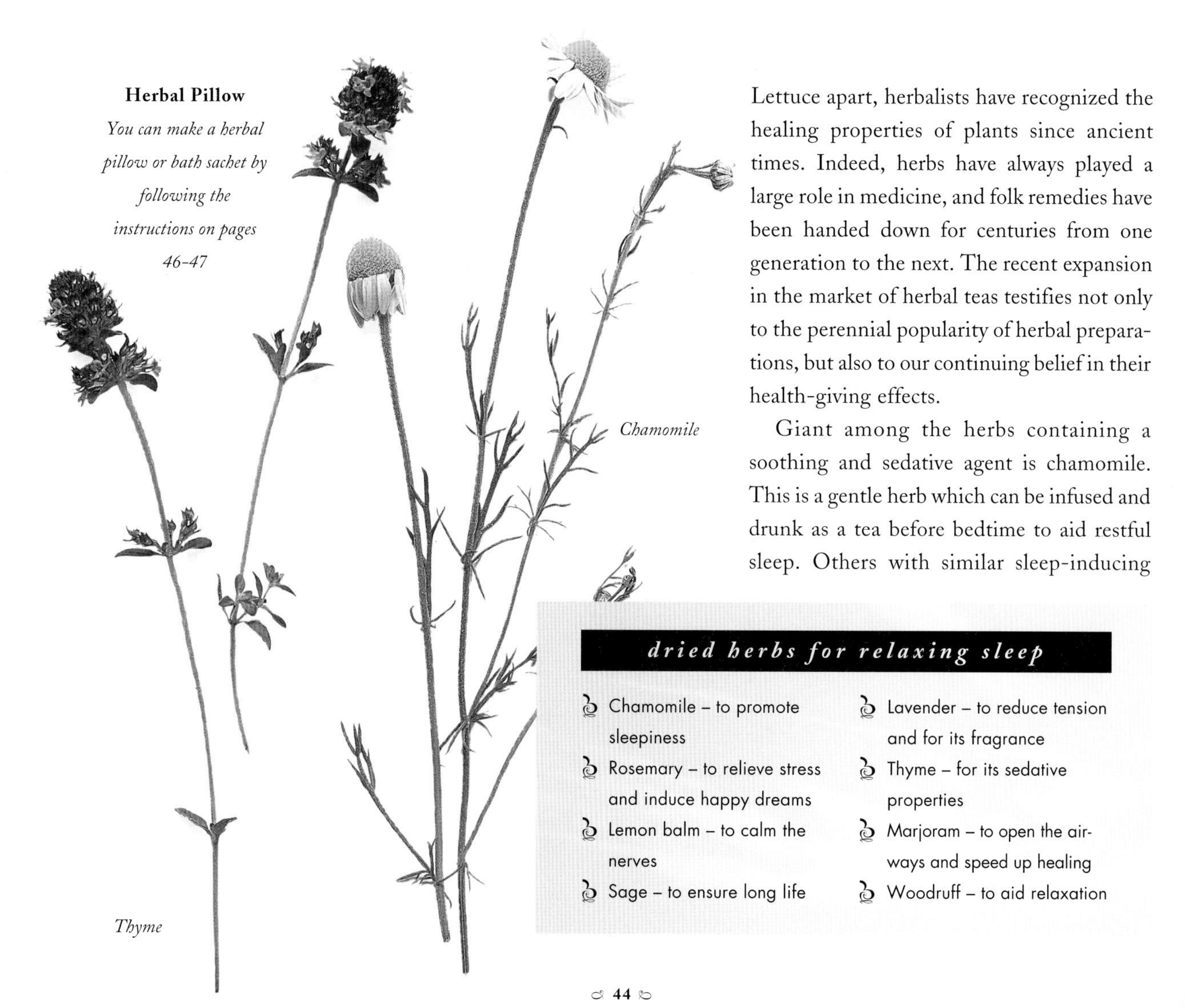

Herbal Pillow

You can make a herbal pillow or bath sachet by following the instructions on pages 46–47

Chamomile

Thyme

Lettuce apart, herbalists have recognized the healing properties of plants since ancient times. Indeed, herbs have always played a large role in medicine, and folk remedies have been handed down for centuries from one generation to the next. The recent expansion in the market of herbal teas testifies not only to the perennial popularity of herbal preparations, but also to our continuing belief in their health-giving effects.

Giant among the herbs containing a soothing and sedative agent is chamomile. This is a gentle herb which can be infused and drunk as a tea before bedtime to aid restful sleep. Others with similar sleep-inducing

dried herbs for relaxing sleep

- Chamomile – to promote sleepiness
- Rosemary – to relieve stress and induce happy dreams
- Lemon balm – to calm the nerves
- Sage – to ensure long life
- Lavender – to reduce tension and for its fragrance
- Thyme – for its sedative properties
- Marjoram – to open the airways and speed up healing
- Woodruff – to aid relaxation

properties include rosemary, lavender, marjoram, and lemon balm. Dried and mixed together, these plants can be made into herbal pillows or sewn into individual sachets and added to a warm bath just before bed.

SCENTED SACHETS

Scented sachets have been used throughout history for a variety of reasons. Sometimes they were carried both as a form of personal deodorant and as a counter to unpleasant environmental smells. Sachets filled with lavender were, and still are, slipped into cupboards and drawers to scent the linen and to protect against moths. Herbal cushions or pillows have also been used for many years to relieve stress and to help people fall asleep.

Herbal remedy
Drinking herbal tea or using a herb pillow can have a sedative effect

HOW TO MAKE A HERBAL PILLOW

Herbs have been used for centuries to aid sleep. Some herbs are renowned for their dream-enhancing properties, and in the past they were strewn around beds and on floors. A herbal pillow is a comfortable way to enjoy the special powers of herbs. You can choose any of the herbs from the list on p44, but why not experiment with different combinations? To find which herbs give you the happiest reveries, you could make several herb pillows with varying mixtures of herbs, and try a different one each night.

You will need

FOR CUSHION

Fabric approx 2ft 3in x 12in (65 x 30cm)
Matching thread
Coloured ribbon 4ft (120cm)
Kapok for stuffing

FOR HERB SACHET

2 pieces of muslin 6in x 8in (15cm x 24cm)
White thread
Dried herbs: thyme chamomile, rosemary, lavender, lemon balm

Soothing nights
A pillow filled with soporific herbs will lull you gently into your dreamworld

instructions to make a herbal pillow

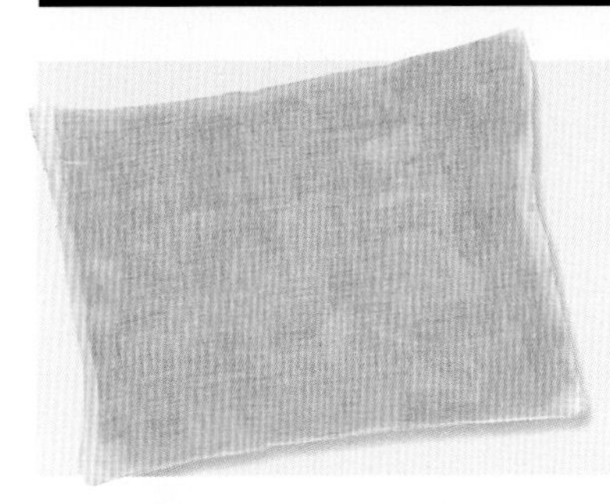

To make the herb sachet

- *Place together the two pieces of muslin and sew around the three sides, leaving one side open. Turn inside out and press. Fill with a selection of dried herbs from the suggestions opposite. Slip stitch the opening and the sachet is ready to be inserted into the finished cushion.*

To make the cushion

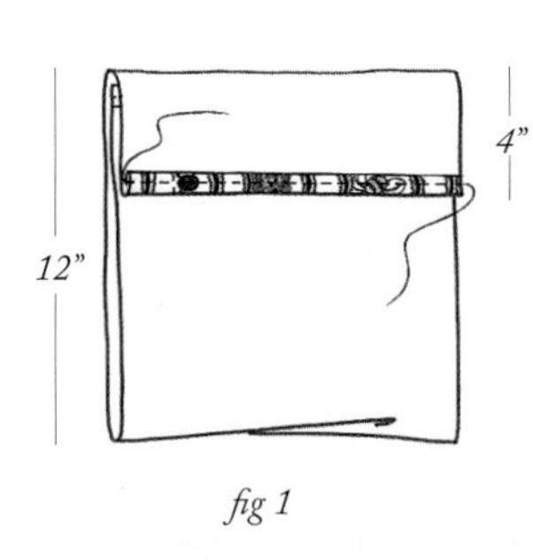

fig 1

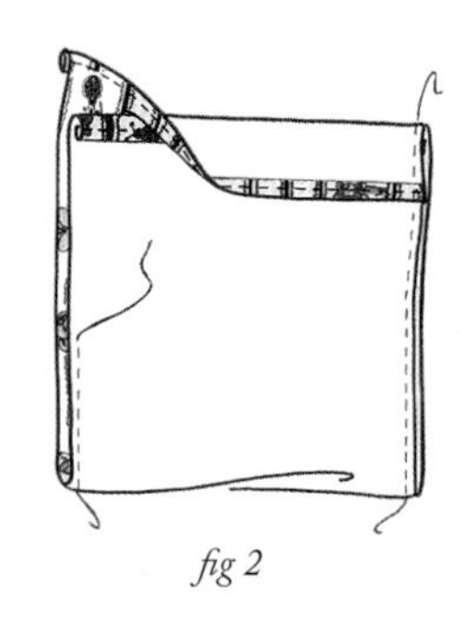

fig 2

FIGURE 1

- *Turn and hem the two short edges of fabric (12in 30cm edges). With right side facing inwards, fold the fabric as shown in the diagram, making sure to leave an overlapping flap of 4in (10cm).*

FIGURE 2

- *Taking a ½in (1cm) seam allowance, pin together side seams. Stitch down seams, continuing through the three thicknesses at the flap overlap.*

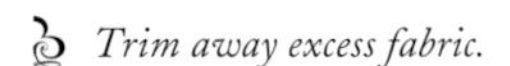

- *Trim away excess fabric.*
- *Turn right-side out and press.*
- *The flap should now be on the inside.*
- *Working on the wrong side, sew three sides together.*
- *Turn right-side out.*

FIGURE 3

- *Cut the ribbon into four equal lengths to make two pairs. Pin each pair of ribbons to top of cushion on either side of the opening, 2¼in (4cm) in from the outside edges. Secure each ribbon with two rows of stitching. Trim ribbons by cutting a deep V-notch into each end.*

FIGURE 4

- *Fill cushion with kapok, inserting the herb sachet into the centre, and tucking the stuffing behind the inside flap.*

FIGURE 5

- *Pin together across top of opening and slip stitch to close.*

FIGURE 6

- *Complete by tying ribbons into pretty bows. Keep your herb cushion beside you whenever you sleep or nap.*

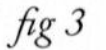

fig 3

fig 4

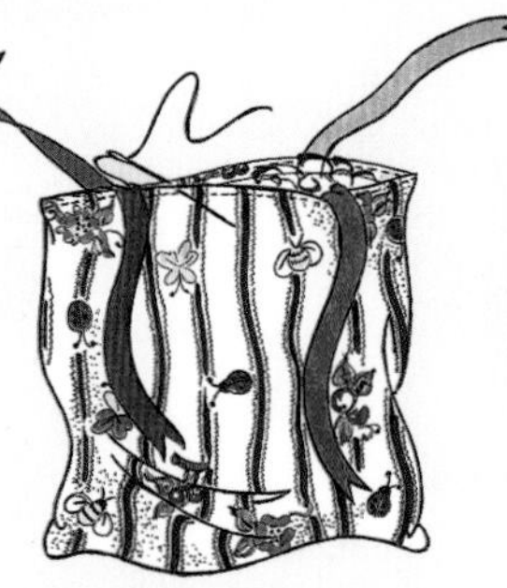

fig 5

fig 6

GEMSTONES AND CRYSTALS

The healing power of crystals has been known by sages for thousands of years. Each stone emits an energy field that works upon our own energies and thus corrects and equalizes any vibrational imbalances in our systems. In this way crystals can make us feel better.

Of course, as well as their healing properties, crystals and gemstones are fabulous objects in their own right. They range in color from the deepest purples of the amethyst, through the intense crimson of the ruby, to the dazzling white of the diamond. Some are opalescent, while others are as clear and transparent as a mountain stream. Don't think you need to spend a fortune on your stones – because a lovely chunk of rock crystal or a piece of quartz are fairly inexpensive – but, if they work for you, they can be powerfully effective.

Each stone performs a different type of magic. Some crystals absorb our negative feelings, others have a rejuvenating effect. Some should be carried in a pocket so that they are close to the body or can be held next to the skin. Those, however, that are placed under a pillow or on the bedside table will help you relax and induce sweet dreams as you sleep.

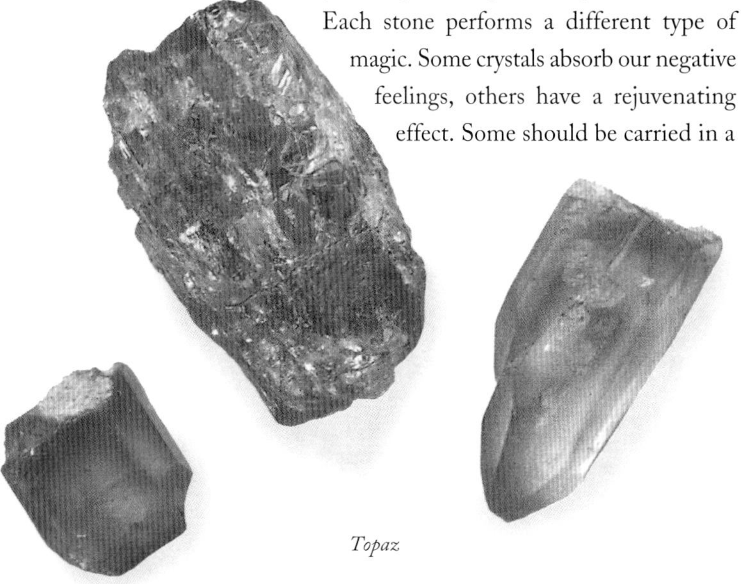

Topaz

CHOOSING YOUR CRYSTAL

Crystals "tune in" to different people, and that is why you will be attracted to certain stones and not to others. Perhaps the best way to purchase your crystal is simply to choose the one you like best.

PERSONALIZING YOUR STONE

Once you have chosen your stone, you will need to personalize it. Wash it under running water to clear the energies it has absorbed from other people and leave it outside in the open air or on a window sill for a whole day to recharge itself with light. Now, take your stone to your bedroom, hold it in your hand and meditate. Think of its power and its energy, and feel its vibrations radiating outwards and filling your room with their healing and their gentle peace. Place it by your bedside and it will continue to release its therapeutic energies for you while you sleep.

BEDSIDE BENEFITS

Appropriate crystals and gemstones to place by the bedside in order to create a field conducive to soothing sleep and happy dreams include:

Amethyst

AMETHYST

A wonderful stone with a wide range of powers and one of the best for promoting sleep. Combining red with blue in its color, it coordinates brain activity with the nervous system and has a direct balancing and uplifting effect as you sleep. Moreover, it is valued for its protective powers and it absorbs radiation, which is all the better if your bedroom doubles as an office or if you have a computer close by. Amethysts have a calming effect and soothe emotional excitability. You could place this stone close to your bed or even under your pillow.

QUARTZ

With a piece of milky or snowy quartz, you will fill your sleep with peace and tranquillity. Rose quartz, especially, brings peace to the heart. It is particularly beneficial at times of emotional turmoil and brings comfort after a broken romance. Put it under the pillow or hold it next to your skin.

Quartz crystal

AGATE

A soothing stone that is said to heal an aching head. Moss agates are great destressers, as they calm anxieties and help in times of emotional upset.

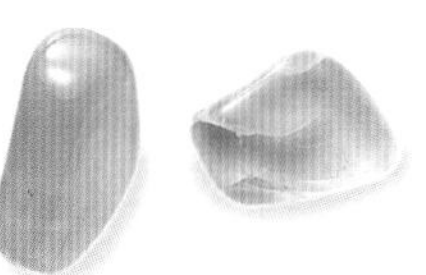

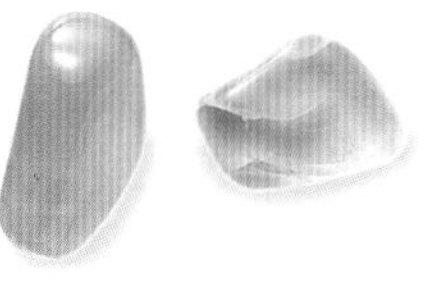

Moonstone

Agate

MOONSTONE

Ruled by the Moon and therefore a stone of the night, the moonstone rules lovers and is said to heighten passion. If your want to identify your future partner, put one by your bedside and before you fall asleep ask your unconscious to show you your true sweetheart in your dreams. This is particularly effective on the nights of the new or full moon.

TOPAZ

Topaz is another great destresser and rebalances the nervous system. All golden stones will give energy and revitalize you as you sleep. Like the amethyst, this is invaluable either by your bedside or under your pillow because it counteracts insomnia and night terrors.

EMERALD

Known as the stone of tranquillity, the emerald not only promotes sleep, but has a reputation for encouraging kindness and a caring instinct. Put an emerald in your bedroom to calm a troubled mind.

AROMATHERAPY

The Egyptian queen, Cleopatra, in preparation for her meetings with Mark Antony, would order her slaves to strew the floor of her bedchamber ankle-deep with rose petals. She knew that the fragrance of roses is soothing and relaxing. But she also knew that, when crushed underfoot, roses release essential oils that are powerful aphrodisiacs.

The practice of using aromatics was widespread among the ancient Egyptians as far back as 3,000 B.C.E. Their knowledge of the properties of plants was extensive, and herbs and flowers were cultivated not so much for their beauty, but more for their healing qualities. Physicians and high priests, especially, understood the therapeutic benefits of plant fragrances and essential oils, and they made great use of both in their medicines and in their religious ceremonies.

Much of our present day knowledge about aromatherapy has been handed down to us from those ancient times. We, in our modern stress-filled world, possibly have an even greater need now for the therapeutic effects of essential oils than our Egyptian, Persian, Greek, or Roman predecessors had in their less industrialized lives. This is because, apart from their curative powers, aromatherapy oils also offer us psychological healing which has proven remarkably effective. Some oils, for example, are potent tonics that can revitalize our spirits, pick us up when we are down and restore our mind-body equilibrium. Others, as Cleopatra knew, stimulate the senses, sharpen our appetites, and enhance our pleasure receptors. Yet others work in the opposite direction, calming anxiety, easing nervous tension and promoting deep and relaxing sleep.

ESSENTIAL OILS TO AID SLEEP

Some of the most useful essential oils amongst the aromatics specifically renowned for their calming and soothing properties are chamomile, lavender, melissa, and rose. For sedative purposes use melissa (which slows the pulse), patchouli, and ylang-ylang – this last oil should be used sparingly, as its intensely sweet fragrance can cause headaches. Neroli is a great destresser and petitgrain will ease tension and depression. Vertiver, known as the oil of tranquillity, is especially calming and soothes nervous tension. Chamomile will make you sleepy and, along with rose, mandarin, and sandal-wood, form part of the group of essential oils used to combat insomnia.

But let's not forget those with aphrodisiac properties, since lovemaking is also essential to our spiritual contentment and well-being. These include rose, neroli, sandalwood, and cedarwood, although this latter oil is not recommended for use in pregnancy.

There are three methods of using these oils, all of which are conducive to relaxation and sleep: bathing, inhalation, and massage.

FOR BATHING

A few drops of either a single oil, or two or three in combination (never combine more than three together) may be added to a warm bath, preferably an hour before bed. Try patchouli, lavender, and rose for a sensual delight that will relax both your mind and your body. Or chamomile, vertiver, and neroli for relaxing sleep and sweet dreams.

FOR INHALATION

Inhaling aromatic oils can also relieve stress, calm the spirits, soothe away worries, promote sleep, and induce dreams. Put two drops of oil in a ceramic dish or sprinkle some on a piece of gauze and place on a radiator to fill the room with therapeutic fragrance. Frankincense lends itself particularly well to being vaporized in this way, and it will also aid meditation. A few drops of lavender sprinkled on the pillow is also useful against insomnia.

FOR MASSAGE

Massage must surely be the most sensual use to which we can put essential oils. But remember, never use pure, undiluted oils straight on the skin. Either buy them ready mixed or mix them yourself with a medium, otherwise known as a carrier oil. Sweet almond, jojoba, or sunflower oil make excellent carrier oils. For massaging purposes, choose any of the oils already mentioned, and add between six to twelve drops of either a single oil or a mixture of two or three of these to a bottle or jar containing 4floz of carrier oil. When massaging, use gentle but firm strokes and always massage *toward* the heart.

Healing herbs
Essential oils extracted from herbs can give sensual pleasure and aid relaxation

part three

THE KEY TO YOUR DREAMWORLD

on home ground

BUILDINGS

If you recognize your own house, or even your own neighborhood in a dream, the chances are that it is a factual dream, picking up on events that have recently taken place in and around your own locality. Or perhaps the action, being centered on familiar territory, carries a message directly concerning your own household. Dream researchers, however, almost unanimously agree that buildings, and a house in particular, represents the dreamer and symbolizes his or her body, personality, or state of mind.

Home truths
The type of house you see in your dream reflects an aspect of you

HOUSES

The architecture or type of house you see in your dream may be a reflection of yourself, of your own image or of the position you hold in life. You may be romantic and therefore associate yourself with a cottage; industrious and thus see yourself as a factory; or rich and successful and depicted by a mansion. A hint to spruce up your appearance may come from an untidy facade, or from decorators refurbishing the property. Watching builders excavating foundations implies a need to prepare your groundwork in order to "ground" yourself or to provide strong, solid roots on which to base a relationship. If you see yourself leaving the house, or if it is up for sale, it may be that you are moving on or making a fresh start in life. Returning to a house you once inhabited may be a device to show you how much you have changed or developed in the intervening years.

SHOPS

In offering a variety of merchandise, a dream shop is reminding you that choices have to be made in your waking life.

CASTLES

Fortresses are places of security and defence. Think of these allusions if you dream about a castle. Perhaps this is a reminder to check your locks or burglar alarms. Or perhaps it is telling you that you are behaving overly defensive and thereby unnecessarily shutting others out of your life.

PLACES OF WORSHIP

Churches, cathedrals, mosques, temples, or other religious places bring to the fore the spiritual side of life. This dream may be reminding you of the need to develop your spirituality, or to look within to your own inner growth. It may also be highlighting the importance of considering the moral implications of a particular situation.

LIBRARIES, SCHOOLS, AND UNIVERSITIES

As repositories of knowledge, dreams that feature these institutions may be encouraging you to seek further information about a certain matter. Alternatively, since they are also places where ideas are exchanged, they could be prompting you to put your thinking cap on or to talk things through with wiser or more informed individuals. Schools imply that in order to make significant spiritual or emotional progress, some valuable lessons may need to be learned.

MUSEUMS

Objects on display refer to your self-image, so this dream will give you clues as to how you appear to others. If the museum itself is old-fashioned or its exhibits are dull, it may be a hint to update your style or to enliven the presentation of yourself.

HOSPITALS

Since hospitals are places of healing, to see one in your dreams might be a message about your health. Perhaps you have been working too hard and this is telling you to take things easy. Meeting someone you know in the hospital may be bringing to your attention your anxieties in waking life about that person's state of health.

STATIONS

Stations, bus terminals, and airport buildings are essentially collecting places, where people come together and then disperse to other destinations. So, in a dream, these buildings may represent a forum for ideas, possibly a meeting of people or of minds. A station may also symbolize that you are on the verge of change, about to take a new direction in life. If it is an airport, it might be that a new venture is "taking off" for you, or that you are about to pursue a long-held goal.

Dream home
Revisiting former haunts can demonstrate how much you've changed over the years

on home ground

ROOMS

In your dreams, the rooms of a house represent aspects of your personality or parts of your anatomy. Consider the roof as symbolizing your head, the facade as the image you present to the outside world, and the various floors as the different levels of your understanding and achievement.

ATTIC

Sited at the top of the house, the attic represents the mind and the higher aspirations. Action centered here in your dream concerns your ideas, hopes, and ambitions. If the attic is crammed with junk, it may indicate that you are becoming narrow-minded – it could be time to review your opinions and to spruce up your ideas. An attic that is completely empty could be suggesting that you need a new interest or that you are ready for fresh developments in your life.

A head for heights
The room at the top of the house reflects the mind and ideas

LIVING ROOM

It is in the living room where we relax after a hard day's work. Dreaming of this room may, on one hand, suggest that you need to relax and unwind more. On the other, if you have been too laid back of late, the dream may encourage you to make more effort.

STAIRS

Like corridors, stairs are linking devices, but, unlike corridors, which link on the same level, stairs take us up a flight and thus to higher things. Ascending a flight of stairs, then, brings in the notion of rising above our present situation. It may imply that with some thought we can find a way out of difficulties, or it may symbolize a rise to success. The steeper the stairs, the more effort we must put in to achieve our desired goal. In general, climbing dreams are associated with a desire to learn more, to reach higher, and to gain greater understanding and better mastery over our skills.

CORRIDOR

Access from one room to another is through a corridor, so, consequently, a corridor may be seen as a go-between or a link of some sort. Perhaps, then, walking through a corridor symbolizes a transitional stage either between periods of personal growth, or between two distinct phases of your life. The room that you reach next will give clues to the developments you may shortly expect in your daily life.

KITCHEN AND DINING ROOM

Because the kitchen is the room where food is prepared, in dreams this often represents the nurturing side of our nature. Kitchens are considered the center of the home and the dining room is where the family comes together to share food at mealtimes – food symbolizing physical and spiritual nourishment. These rooms traditionally describe the current domestic situation. If they are cluttered or messy, complications or difficulties within the family are suggested, and perhaps it is time to thrash things out, have a clean up or in some way clear the air. Contentment and family harmony may be reflected by a warm, cozy kitchen, food on the table, or a cat curled up by the fire.

Family values
A tidy kitchen shows that family life is running calmly and smoothly

BASEMENT

Dream researchers agree that dreams about cellars, basements, or dungeons are commenting on the dark recesses of the unconscious mind. This is where we discover clues about our fears and anxieties, about those aspects of ourselves that we cannot, or will not, recognize, or those inherent skills and talents that are still undeveloped. To enter a dark basement suggests you are tapping your hidden resources and that you are ready to explore those areas of your psyche which have, so far, lain dormant.

on home ground

FURNITURE

It is common for a dream to be set in our own homes and to feature items of furniture that we see and use every day. But no matter how familiar or commonplace they may seem to us, in a dream these household items play a key role in setting the scene, in jogging our memories, or in conveying important information through their symbolic meaning.

Most significant are the items of furniture that are out of place in our dreams, that appear broken or of a different color from their counterparts in our own possession. Such discrepancies as these function to focus the mind on aspects of our lives that may require attention.

Table a motion
A table, and any objects upon it, can be a prompt to take serious action

CLUTTER

If your dream house contains far more furniture than your real home, or if you are trying to cram more furniture into a room than will actually fit, it could be a hint that you have taken on too many commitments. Cleaning up or moving furniture out may be suggesting that you need to off-load, delegate, or sort things out. Throwing away an item of furniture implies it is now time to discard something (or someone) that is no longer of use to you in your life.

TABLE

Do you need to "table a motion" or "draw up a table" at work? If so, dreaming of your own table or desk may be a simple reminder. The message of the dream may lie in whatever is on the table. Greetings or playing cards, for example, could suggest it is time you spoke up or "put your cards on the table." Scissors may imply a need to "cut out" bad habits, especially dietary ones if the scissors are on a dining table. A table laid with glittering silver cutlery may foretell of good fortune coming your way.

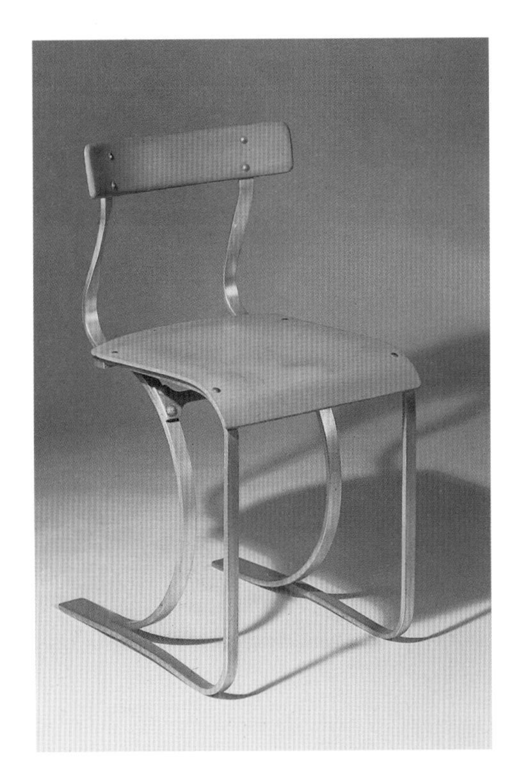

The hot seat
A single isolated chair could be a sign that you are being put on the spot

A bowl of flowers depicts happiness and hope, but if the flowers are fading or shedding their petals, watch out for disappointments and regrets. A cracked table-top may symbolize a break of some kind – with the past, with a tradition, or with a person – or it can draw your attention to a flaw in your argument or in your character.

CHAIR

A soft chair predicts comfort and ease – perhaps an onerous duty will turn out to be easier to perform than you imagine. A hard chair, though, may be warning of a difficult or uncomfortable situation ahead. But if, in your waking life, there is a chair that is favored by a particular person or even a pet in your household, dreaming of that item may be representing not the chair itself, but the person or pet who regularly sits in that chair.

BED

There are obvious sexual connotations when a bed appears in a dream. Otherwise, a bed may symbolize warmth, comfort, or security. A bed strewn with flowers might bring to mind the expression, "a bed of roses," suggesting an easy life. A hard bed, however, may be a reflection of a difficult life.

Rank and file
Neat rows might suggest that there is something you would like to put in order

CLOSETS AND DRESSERS

Items of furniture such as dressers are essentially receptacles, and the message of the dream may be found in the contents, or in the lack of contents, as the case may be. Lacy underwear, for example, adds an erotic theme, while cupboards that are bare may suggest emotional emptiness or financial difficulties, depending on the context. Locked drawers indicate secrets or misunderstandings.

on home ground

DOORS AND WINDOWS

Dreams that feature doors are highly significant, for they can represent entrances, openings, opportunities, and new beginnings. Consider some of the expressions we use that involve doors: "open door policy," "laying the blame at one's door," "when one door closes, another one opens." Windows, too, are important dream symbols, often synonymous with viewing or with sight. Sayings in modern usage containing the word "window" include: "the eyes are the window of the soul," "mere window-dressing," and "out of the window," a colloquialism that means that something is no longer relevant.

OPEN DOORS VERSUS CLOSED DOORS

An open door in your dream is a classic symbol of invitation, and it bids you to enter. Doors in dreams symbolize new developments. They stand, like a rite of passage, between you and the next phase in your life and what they open before you is possibility. Perhaps this may symbolize a new job, or leaving home to start an independent life, or moving to a different country. For a woman, it might mark the beginning of the menopause or, for an employee, it could signify the end of working life and the beginning of retirement.

Sometimes, the open door symbolizes the opportunity to discover more about oneself, to develop latent talents, or to analyze parts of one's personality that have lain dormant. If, in your dream, you choose to walk through the door, it means you are ready to accept the challenges that are before you in your daily life. If you demur, it could mean you are not ready, or that you are afraid to face what is ahead of you.

The same may be true if the door before you is closed. Here, it is possible that you are not ready or that the opportunity you had

Curtain call
Closed curtains hide an unpleasant state of affairs or conceal a secret

hoped for is not yet available for you. If you deliberately close the door, it could mean that you choose not to take that step forward, that you are not prepared to make the necessary changes that are being asked of you. Alternatively, and on a personal level, it may be suggesting that you want to close yourself off from other people.

FIXTURES AND FITTINGS

A door that is locked and will not permit entry implies that something is being withheld from you. Seeing the lock without a key suggests frustrations, or that you cannot, for some reason, find the answer to your problems. As in waking life, a key in a dream is the solution. Turning the key in the lock is a positive action and a statement of readiness for whatever is next in store. This also implies you will soon find the answer you have been seeking. Focusing on a mailbox is connected with communications. Perhaps you will soon be receiving news. If there is a number on the door, take note, as the message of the dream may lie in that number's symbolism. Door handles, when emphasized, suggest you need to get a grip on the situation.

WINDOWS

If you are looking at a window, could this be a "window of opportunity." Whatever you see through the dream window will give you an insight into what you can expect to happen next in your waking hours. A garden full of lush vegetation is a sign of hope, whereas rubble would warn of disappointments and failed plans. Seeing a brick wall, however, could denote limitations. Take another look – is there a gate or a set of steps that might offer you a way out?

Room with a view
The view through a window presages events to come in waking life

CURTAINS

The action of drawing curtains together effectively blocks something out, and in a dream this either suggests you have a secret or that you are refusing to face up to a situation in everyday life. The scene through the window that is being screened off will give a clue to whatever it is you are unwilling to confront. Drawing back the curtains, on the other hand, means that you want to look out, to face the world, to see your destiny. The scene the open curtains expose will give you the clues to what lies ahead.

on home ground

RECEPTACLES

Eclectic as this collection of images may appear, receptacles share a common purpose, which is to hold, or provide storage for, other objects. As such, this theme presents an interesting category of dreams, since containers of all kinds offer scope for a rich variety of symbolism on many levels. The message of the dream may be conveyed simply by the receptacle itself. Alternatively, the container may be used as a vehicle, the significance lying in its fabric, shape, color or contents.

BAGS AND BAGGAGE

Heavy load
Bags and baskets can contain thoughts and problems, or even hidden talents

On a factual level, you may dream of an assortment of bags and suitcases if you are planning a journey or if you have been making travel arrangements. If you use a specific bag for your work, a briefcase for a lecturer, say, or a medical bag for a physician, the bag itself may represent your job. But in dreams, baggage often symbolizes our commitments and responsibilities, the thoughts and problems that we carry around with us every day. A dream in which you are carrying heavy bags may be alluding to the fact that you feel overburdened – practically or emotionally – in your waking life. Perhaps you are taking on too much and your unconscious is now advising you to offload in some way. Carrying a bag with ease, however, suggests that you are coping comfortably with the demands in your life.

What is in the bag? Money or other valuables could refer to your material assets or else they may denote hidden talents. Depending on the rest of the action, taking something out of the bag, therefore, either implies a demand on your personal resources or a wish to develop a latent skill. Putting something into a bag may refer to an acquisition of a material, intellectual, or spiritual nature. On quite a different level, bags are said to symbolize the female sexual organs, so that slipping an object into a purse, for example, may imply sexual intercourse.

BOXES AND CHESTS

Boxes are fascinating dream images not only because they are containers, but, more importantly, because very often they are fitted with a lock and key. Tipping out a box full of junk could be your unconscious telling you it is time to have a clear out. This might imply spring cleaning or redecorating your house. Or perhaps, on a physical level, it may be encouraging you to make personal changes, to try a new image, or go on a cleansing diet. Intellectually, you might consider taking up a new course of study, learning something that will be of value to you in your life or career. If, in opening the box, you find it is full of treasure, take it as an endorsement of your attributes. A box that is locked, though, suggests a secret; perhaps there is something you would rather not reveal. Maybe someone is keeping something from you, or there is something you do not understand. Finding the key and unlocking the box refers to finding an answer or a solution to a current problem that you have.

SAFES

Safes are associated with security. Whatever is kept in your dream safe will symbolize something in your life that you value and either wish to protect, or are being advised to safeguard.

If it is money, perhaps you should think about your long term investments or try to put your finances on a firmer footing. Documents may represent projects or ideas that you need to protect against competitors. Other valuables may stand for personal attributes that need shielding, such as your integrity or good name.

Bottled up

A stoppered bottle is a heavy hint about your current emotional state

GLASS CONTAINERS

Because glass is transparent, a dream about a vase or a bottle may be a device that comments on your perspicacity. A jam jar full of earth, for example, might reflect your attempts to solve a mystery – that is, trying to penetrate into something dark. Looking through a crystal vase says that you have clear vision. On a different level, a bottle with a firm stopper may hint at "bottled up" emotions. But drinking from a glass suggests spiritual refreshment.

loved ones and important events

THE FAMILY

How do you see your family? As a closely knit group of people who love and care about each other, or as a hot-bed of competitive egos bickering constantly amongst themselves? Your own experiences of family life and your attitudes to individual relatives are critically important, both to the content of your dreams and to their meaning.

A dream about your family or about a particular relation may be interpreted symbolically, each image representing an association of ideas and triggering messages that may have nothing whatsoever to do with the actual character in that dream. Or else the dream is simply picking up on an event that has taken place, allowing you to review it before the memory is filed away. Occasionally though, a family member may be representing an experience or a characteristic – a *spinster* aunt, an *untidy* brother, a *lucky* cousin – that you associate with that particular person or that you recognize in your own personality.

Motherly love
A mother figure in your dreams can give advice or comfort in times of need

HAPPY FAMILIES

Dreams of a happy family, warm and snug in a brightly lit home, augur contentment and well-being. Quarrels amongst the family, however, warn of problems and difficulties to come.

FATHER

As head of the family, a father is often synonymous with authority figures in general and may substitute, in a dream, for a policeman, a boss, a school principal, a judge or even for the president – in short, the one who gives the orders and lays down the law. If your relationship with your own father was good, you are likely to dream of him as a benign figure. But if he was strict and authoritarian, he might appear in the guise of an ogre or a bear. Apart from a symbol of power, a father may also represent guidance, justice, and protection.

MOTHER

In dream lore, a mother represents the feminine principle or women in general. Because she gives life, she stands for protec-

tion and nurturing. By extension, she may also symbolize nature or Mother Earth. Mothers offer tenderness, wisdom, and support, and may appear in our dreams when we are in need of comfort and consolation. If your mother speaks, she may give words of advice or she may act as our consciences, admonishing us over our misdeeds as when we were children.

BROTHER

Apart from appearing as himself in your dreams, a brother may substitute for a close friend, a male partner, or a rival; otherwise he may symbolize the universal brotherhood of man.

Fighting with your brother in a dream may be a warning of impending arguments in your waking life. Dreaming that he is in danger may be another type of advance warning of a real event, or it could arise because of a personal anxiety about his welfare in real life.

SISTER

Sisters in dreams may substitute for girl-friends or female acquaintances, sometimes even for wives or lovers. Alternatively, she may symbolize the feminine and emotional side of your personality. Dreaming about your own sister may simply bring to your attention an aspect of her behavior, or it may replay an incident that occurred when you were last together. If she speaks, perhaps she is giving you sisterly advice. You may be "tuning in" to her emotions or getting a glimpse of a future incident that will affect her. Interestingly, your unconscious may use wordplay in your dream and substitute a nun in place of your own sister, or vice versa.

GRANDPARENTS

In dreams, grandparents often represent maturity and wisdom.

A family affair

Dreams of harmonious family life indicate happiness and contentment

loved ones and important events

LOVERS AND IDOLS

As the song says, "Love is a many splendored thing," and in our dreams our feelings of love may be symbolized in many different ways. Dream love and lovers serve a variety of functions from confirming our affections to satisfying the most improbable fantasies of our waking lives.

ROMANTIC LOVE

Many dreams containing scenes of romance fall into the category of wish-fulfillment. Broken love affairs, for example, are soon mended in our dreams, old flames are revisited, lost lovers return to our sides, promises of undying affection are pledged anew. These themes play an invaluable therapeutic role in our lives since they not only act as a vehicle through which we can release our tension, but in them we are also allowed to enjoy the pleasures and the gratification we may be missing in our day-to-day lives.

True love
The fears and uncertainties of actual relationships can be overcome in your dreams

DREAM LOVERS

Also in the wish-fulfillment category are those nighttime reveries in which we meet and court our dream lovers - the heroes and heroines of our imagination, the knights in shining armor, the fair damsels in distress, or else the idols of the silver screen and the pin-ups who fill our thoughts during the day. If you have a real-life partner who reminds you of a rock star or of a famous actor, your unconscious may substitute one for the other in your dreams.

Of course, if you have just fallen in love, it is not unusual to dream of your new lover in the guise of a dashing prince or in the form of a beautiful princess, for this indeed is how your beloved appears to you in your conscious mind.

THE KISS

Wishful thinking or factual replay? And, for that matter, who in your dream is kissing whom? Affectionate kisses between relatives often represent joy and contentment in your emotional life at the moment. Long, lingering, passionate kisses between you and your partner reflect the love and desire you have for one another. But, if you are currently in a relationship and you dream that you are kissing a person you recognize who is not your partner, it may be a sign that you are bored with your present situation and you're beginning to think it is time to move on. Seeing your real-life partner kissing someone else in a dream could be highlighting your feelings of jealousy. Or could this be a prompt from your unconscious, bringing fully to your attention those half-formed suspicions, or putting together little tell-tale signs of infidelity that you refused to accept with your waking eyes?

THE EMBRACE

Being wrapped in the embrace of someone you know is confirmation that you are loved and cherished. To feel that you have protective arms around you is also a sign of reassurance, a device where your unconscious lets you know that you are safe, or tells you that you have a guardian angel watching over you. To hug yourself in a dream is a positive way to build your self-esteem and to acknowledge your strengths and talents. A dream lover's tender embrace must surely be one of the most comforting images we could ever wish to experience in our dreams.

Romantic impulse
Dreaming of an illicit love affair might suggest that you are bored with your current relationship

loved ones and important events

BIRTH AND DEATH

Dreams about the birth of a baby or the death of an individual rank among some of the most common themes in dream records. And yet, unless the dreamer is an experienced psychic, these hardly ever foretell a real birth or an actual death. Rich in symbolism, they more usually occur at a time of change in our lives, predicting a turning point or a breakthrough in our affairs.

Life events

Dreams of birth or death are usually psychological or spiritual in nature

BABIES AND BIRTH

For a pregnant woman, dreaming about giving birth is a factual dream and is part of the unconscious process of preparing for the event. However, on a symbolic level, and for those who are not expectant parents, babies represent ideas, inherent gifts, talents, and potential. Just as giving birth in waking life is an act of creation, so it is in dreams, as giving birth signifies the process of giving life to a new idea, a new project, or a venture that has been incubating in the dreamer's mind for some time. Strong feelings of love and desire to nurture and protect a baby in one's dreams may indeed refer to the real love for one's own child. But these emotions may be interpreted as a love for a new project in hand, and a smiling baby may represent that all is progressing well. Conversely, should the baby cry or annoy the dreamer, it suggests that all is not going as it should and reflects problems and irritations in waking life.

To dream of a premature baby suggests the time is not yet right to launch the new venture. Better to think through the idea some more, and wait until it has developed into a sounder proposition before launching it into the world. If the baby takes a few steps, it is an encouraging sign that the new venture "has legs," or shows potential.

CHILDREN

Aspects of our own children's personalities or insights into their behavior may be brought to our attention in factual dreams that feature our own offspring. Otherwise, children in our dreams symbolize our hopes and aspirations for the future. Happy children show our confidence about the progress of our lives and careers, whereas sad children suggest that our outlook is tinged with pessimism. The juxtaposition of a child and an adult may act as a symbolic comparison, asking us to consider youth versus maturity, or highlighting the differences between intuition and logic, between naivety and wisdom.

DEATH

Disturbing as a dream about death may be, like dreams of birth, these usually predict changes. Occasionally, however, they may reflect our anxieties about someone we know, especially if we have been concerned about that person's health and well-being in real life. On a different level, dreams of death, whether one's own or another's, foretell a transformation or transition, a time of new beginnings, a rebirth, and a new phase that is about to begin, often challenging. These dreams encourage us to see our true potential and accept the need for considerable psychological and spiritual change or growth.

FUNERALS, BURIALS AND GRAVEYARDS

Watching a macabre film before bed can often trigger dreams about funerals and graveyards. Symbolically, however, to dream of a burial may be a gentle hint that it is time to bury the past, to come to terms with events and move on. Like drowning, the image of being buried alive may reflect pressures bearing down on us in our lives. Physically, too, a late dinner may induce this type of dream, producing as it does a feeling of heaviness on the stomach.

Somber signals
Dreams of death suggest a need to come to terms with our own mortality

loved ones and important events

FUN AND FESTIVITIES

Parties, celebrations, and having fun with our friends and family are all occasions that can raise the spirits. Laughter, we now recognize, has enormous therapeutic value, providing a tonic that can instantly lift our moods and make us feel physically as well as psychologically better.

Frivolity
Dancing shows your life is full and busy

Judging from our dreams, the unconscious mind, too, it would appear, enjoys a sense of humor. It likes using puns in our dreams, amusingly presenting us with information that can be interpreted on any number of levels, or else it teases us by wrapping the message around a play on words. Indeed, a dream that is being recounted all too often sounds like something straight out of comedy, or more suited to the theater of the absurd.

It is as well to bear this in mind when analyzing your dreams, but especially so when dealing with those that contain images of entertainment. For, among the more sententious dream symbolism, we must not miss the fact that dreams can also provide a strong element of fun.

BIRTHDAY PARTIES

Are you a guest or the host at this party? Is it lively, full of music and laughter, or does it resemble more of a wake? Dreaming that you are a sparkling host or hostess surrounded by a large group of people, either confirms your popularity or, depending on the context, may be a wish-fulfillment dream highlighting how much you dearly wish you had lots of friends. Happiness, too, may be interpreted both ways, according to your own personal circumstances, either reflecting your own contentment in life, or as a compensation for the sadness you are experiencing. The emotions you feel on waking will provide the key.

On a different level, because birthdays mark a turning point, the message may be one of new beginnings when they feature in a dream, pointing out the end of a particular phase in the dreamer's life and the start of a new one. Dancing and activity at the party could reflect that you have hit a busy time in your life at present, but, since it is at a party, it implies that your efforts are bringing you a good deal of pleasure and satisfaction. If there is a birthday cake, take note of the number and color of the candles because these, too, could be carrying information significant to the interpretation of the dream.

WEDDINGS

Weddings symbolize a union or a merger. Or they may represent the coming together of two people or of two states of being, opposite yet complementary to each other. Such a dream as this, for example, may reflect a business partnership. On a higher level, it may signify the union of conscious and unconscious, or the fusion of the rational with the creative. Alternatively, dreaming of a wedding may be a reminder of other kinds of vows that have been taken and promises that have been made. For single people particularly, the image of a wedding may constitute a wish-fulfillment dream.

RELIGIOUS FESTIVALS

The excitement and anticipation of presents may well induce youngsters to dream about festivals such as Christmas. But behind these times of celebration lies a religious theme that prompts the dreamer to consider the spiritual side of life.

Diwali or Candlemas, however, by introducing the element of light, might signify a breakthrough, a solution to a problem: in short, "seeing the light." Other dreams of celebration, such as Rosh Hashanah or the Chinese Spring festival, which mark the start of the new year, may, like dreams about birthdays, symbolize new beginnings.

Join the party
Carnivals and festivals reflect your sociable side, and can suggest a desire to be part of a group

the body and physical appearance

PARTS OF THE BODY

There are three different levels of interpretation for a dream in which parts of the body appear: physical, symbolic, or as a way of compensating for what you see as your physical failings. Your interpretation very much depends on the circumstances surrounding your life at the time of the dream.

On the physical level, allusions to a particular area of your anatomy may be literally alerting you to a potential health problem in that part of your body. For example, a dream that you're choking on a fish bone may be a warning of an impending sore throat. On a symbolic level, the sensation of choking may be bringing to your attention a problem that is stifling you – too much pressure at work, perhaps, or the effects upon you of a jealous and overprotective lover.

In some cases, we may experience dreams in which the body features prominently to make up for imperfections or disabilities in our own daily lives. Someone who is petite, for instance, may, in a dream, see herself with more ample proportions and as tall as any model on a catwalk. And it is not uncommon for a paraplegic to see himself walking and running in his dreams.

THE HEAD

Seeing a head in your dream may be a unconscious encouragement to be logical about a certain situation: in short, to "use your head." Or this may be prompting you to work harder in order to "get ahead." Alternatively, this dream may be referring to your employer, the head of the organization in which you work, or the principal of a school. If the head is disporportionately large, it may be implying egotistical notions, or overinflated ideas.

THE SHOULDERS

Dreaming that your shoulders hurt, or that you are carrying a heavy weight on your back,

In your own hands
Dreaming of beautiful hands could imply creative success

could be reflecting your present responsibilities. If you can take the weight comfortably then you are on top of things, but if you are bent double under your burden, it could be that your responsibilities are too onerous and that you would be wise to delegate or offload in some way.

THE ARMS

Are you reaching out to someone or are the arms reaching out to you? Outstretched arms indicate a need of some sort – or to be helped, to be hugged, to be accepted.

THE HANDS

Someone with a guilty conscience might dream that his or her hands are dirty, whilst washing one's hands implies renouncing all responsibility for a particular situation. If the index finger is pointing, take notice of what is being shown, as this could convey important information to help you when you awake.

THE LEGS

Think about the expressions we use containing the word leg, and judge whether these might fit the interpretation of your dream. For example, if you have been arguing on a false premise you may not "have a leg to stand on." Or, if you have gone to bed exhausted, you may dream of being "on your last legs." If you are in danger of oversleeping, your unconscious may flash you a dream of running legs in an attempt to urge you to "leg it," and escape.

THE FEET

If you are dragging your feet in your dream, could it be highlighting a certain reluctance in a situation in your waking life? Or perhaps your dream is telling you it's high time you made a bid for independence, to "stand on your own two feet." Experiencing itchy feet in a dream foretells a journey, while cold feet suggests you want to pull out of an agreement.

Feet are associated with walking which, in our dreams, symbolizes the progress we are making in our lives. Striding purposefully tells of confidence in the direction our lives are going, stumbling suggests uncertainty, while shuffling along hints at burdens and heavy responsibilities. Standing still may be alluding to a lack of forward progress or to being stuck in a rut.

Weighty problems
Painful shoulders in dreams suggest your current responsibilities are too much for you

the body and physical appearance

THE FACE

In our waking lives as well as in our dreams, our faces are our "personae," and they represent the image we put across to other people. But, because the face is the most expressive part of the human anatomy, it can also reflect our personality and emotions, communicate in an instant the subtlest mood or feeling, the most fleeting thought or intention without even using a single word.

Face value
A smile on your own face reaffirms your popularity

In your dreams, then, a face – whether it is your own, that of someone you recognize, or one that is completely strange to you – will be communicating a message to you either through its expression, or its appearance.

FACIAL EXPRESSIONS

The expression of the face will give you a clue to the meaning of the dream. For example, a sad face may be picking up on an unhappy event that occurred to you in the day, or it might be warning you of a disappointment ahead. A frowning face may be pointing out that you don't quite understand everything going on in a particular situation in your everyday life. A face with an accusatory look could be your own conscience chastising you for some minor misdeed. This may be doubly emphasized if the face is dirty, showing that you're feeling guilty or ashamed of your actions. A happy, smiling face, of course, is an endorsement of the way things are going in your life and foretells of happiness and good fortune to come.

MOODS

Seeing your own face in a dream may be a reflection of the mood you are giving out to those around you. If you are looking miserable, this could be telling you that others have been finding you bad company of late.

A scowl on your face could mean that your displeasure is making life unpleasant for those who are living or working with you. A mischievous grin may suggest you've been stirring trouble for your friends and colleagues. A happy, smiling face is positive reassurance that others find you a likeable and friendly person to have around.

MASKS

Because we use masks to disguise ourselves or to conceal our true feelings, to see one in your dreams warns of deceit. Who is wearing the mask? If it is covering your own face you may need to question your honesty. If someone you recognize is wearing a mask, it is possible that that person is not all he or she pretends to be. Here, your unconscious is warning you not to place too much trust in this individual.

COSMETICS

Make-up can be considered as a type of mask and may be interpreted in a similar way – as concealment and disguise. Alternatively, because cosmetics are used to enhance the features and to bring color to the face, for a woman to dream about applying make-up implies a desire for a change of image or perhaps recognition that she needs to spruce up her style. To dream that a man you know in waking life is putting on make-up might, in the same way, be suggesting that he is hiding behind a mask, or it could be highlighting his more feminine side – that he is caring or gentle, for example. If you are applying make-up to yourself, note what colors you are using, as these, too, have a symbolic meaning of their own. Lipstick, however, is a special case, because it focuses on the lips and therefore has erotic overtones.

FACES SMALL AND LARGE

What about the actual size of the face in your dream? Was it disproportionately large or did it appear unusually small? Seeing a large face suggests an overinflated ego. If this was your own face, your unconscious may be suggesting that you have been behaving in a rather egotistical fashion.

If your face is too small, on the other hand, could imply that you are shy and too self-effacing for your own good.

Face the facts

The size of your face in a dream reflects your view of yourself

the body and physical appearance

FACIAL FEATURES

While a dream about a face is associated with image, individual features that draw the attention, or that are especially emphasized on the face, will each carry their own symbolic meanings. Moreover, the fact that facial features are linked to the senses increases the opportunity for the unconscious to make use of dream metaphors, puns, and other word-play such as "possessing an ear for music" or "keeping an eye on the situation."

THE EYES

Dreams about eyes are often a comment on how you view your life or situation at the moment. If, for example, your eyes are closed or your sight is dimmed in any way, this may suggest that you are not facing facts, or that you are not seeing the whole truth about a situation in your life. "Be more perceptive and aware" may be the message of a dream in which heavy eyelids are closing over the eyes. And if you see a fleece in front of your face, you should question whether someone is trying to "pull the wool over your eyes."

Blind faith
Regaining sight in a dream can signal a return to childlike innocence

THE EARS

Are you listening to what those around you are trying to tell you? Perhaps you are not taking the advice being offered. Or might you be turning a deaf ear to someone in need? Any of these interpretations might apply to a dream in which ears are especially featured.

THE NOSE

If you have been taking more than a cursory interest in other people's affairs, you might see a nose in your dream bringing to your attention your "nosey aspects." To dream that you are looking down your nose is a hint that you could be condescending, while walking with your nose in the air implies haughtiness.

THE MOUTH

If the mouth speaks, listen carefully to what it says, as it could be giving important information straight from your unconscious. Otherwise, dreams about the mouth may be alluding to either speaking or eating – the twin functions of the mouth – and which one applies would depend on your personal circumstances in your waking life. For example, a dream in which a mouth has been taped over might refer to the fact that you have been given information which you know must be kept strictly confidential. Alternatively, if you are on a diet, the same dream may be offering you motivation.

Hunger pangs

The mouth can suggest a voracious personality which may need taming

THE LIPS

Lips have long been recognized by dream researchers as symbols of the female genitalia, so, figuring strongly in a dream and especially if they are full and luscious, lips suggest sensuality and sexual desire.

THE TEETH

This is a common dream theme that may be interpreted either physically or symbolically. To dream about a toothache, for example, may be reminding you that it is time to see the dentist. Symbolically, teeth that are decayed or that fall out may be a literal "falling out" with a friend or partner. Losing teeth generally signifies the loss of something important in life – a relationship, a good friend, money, or prestige. And, of course, because teeth are cosmetically important to our image, this can also imply a "loss of face." But to dream of beautiful, even teeth suggests a sense of happiness and well-being.

the body and physical appearance

CLOTHES

Intrinsically associated with self-image, clothes, both in waking life as well as in our dreams, impart a good deal of information about the wearer. Our clothes can reflect our position and status in life, hint at our finances and peer group and comment on our preferences and habits. Consequently, since clothes are such rich sources of information, it is important to pay attention to how people are dressed in our dreams, to observe the color and condition of the garments, to note any outstanding details, and to take account of any discrepancies between the person we dream about and how he or she is dressed.

EMPHASIS

Notice, in your dream, whether the focus centers on a particular item of clothing or on a detail of a garment. A raincoat, for example, suggests protection, a need to insulate oneself against adverse conditions. Epaulettes, on the other hand, draw the eye to the shoulders, an allusion to "shouldering" responsibilities. This

Well dressed
New or expensive clothes in a dream suggest pride and self-confidence

detail on a jacket has the effect of broadening the shoulders, thus implying that the dreamer is able to carry the burden of his or her commitments.

CONDITION AND COLOR

The condition of the clothes that you are wearing in your dream will say a good deal about your state of mind. A dirty dress, for instance, may reflect a feeling of shame or disgrace, while a stiffly starched shirt conveys the notion of aloofness and formality. New or expensive-looking clothes reflect confidence, pride, or well-being; the opposite is suggested by ragged, unkempt clothing, which may also imply a lowering of standards. Dreaming that you are wearing clothes that are uncomfortable or too tight suggests you are finding that a situation in your life is rather restrictive – perhaps you feel your freedom is being curtailed or that you are being forced to conform. Brightly colored clothes convey a positive outlook, whereas dull or drab hues may imply that you are suffering from melancholia and depression.

UNSUITABLE ATTIRE

To dream that someone you know is wearing clothes that are quite atypical of him or herself is calling to your attention a discrepancy in that person's character or behavior. If you have had a disagreement with your husband and you dream that he is dressed in school uniform, for example, it suggests that you think he is being immature. Or, if your best friend is wearing a clown's outfit, it could be that you believe he or she is making a fool of themselves in a particular situation in real life. Dreaming that you are inappropriately dressed for an occasion can suggest a fear of making a *faux pas*, or highlight a vulnerability or fear. Turning up at a grand ball in jeans might be one such example, or standing at a bus stop with your skirt tucked into your underpants might be another. This latter example may also be classified as an embarrassment dream.

Image conscious
Dreaming of clothes might suggest a time for a change, to bring a little glamor into your life

A CHANGE OF IMAGE

To dream that you are buying new clothes or trying them on in front of a mirror suggests you feel the need to change your image. Perhaps, on a materialistic level, this dream is implying that it is time you smartened yourself up or updated your wardrobe or hairstyle. Alternatively, and on a more philosophical level, it could be encouraging you to take a look at yourself, your beliefs and values, to consider your progress and, if necessary, to make some relevant changes in your outlook and lifestyle.

the body and physical appearance

ITEMS OF CLOTHING

Individual items of clothing may either directly represent a particular part of the body or draw attention to it, thereby using a pun or a play on words to convey the message of the dream. Shoes, for example, may be interchangeable with feet, or gloves with hands, and expressions such as "handling with kid gloves," or "throwing down the gauntlet," and "footing the bill" are often literally portrayed through the images of clothing in our dreams.

SHOES

Perhaps the most commonly dreamt about items of clothing, shoes have a variety of intriguing interpretations. Associated with walking, they symbolize the progress we are making in our lives. Buying or wearing new shoes foretells a change of direction, a new job, perhaps, or a move. Dreaming that you possess many pairs of shoes could simply be showing you what a busy life you lead, but an inability to choose which pair to put on implies a lack of direction. Losing your shoes can highlight a fear of missing opportunities. Heavy, clumpy shoes that force you to drag your feet reflect difficult or onerous times. But if you are stomping about in hobnail boots, you might question whether you have insensitively trampled over someone's delicate feelings. Shoes with worn heels, alert us to financial restrictions ahead, and unfamiliar shoes signify the need to change your attitude to life. Undone shoelaces could be a reminder to tie up all those loose ends at work.

A head start
If you want to get ahead, get a hat – in dreams, hats symbolize status

HATS

Headwear symbolizes status and position in life, the clue lying in the type of hat that is seen. A crown, for example, is associated with glory and renown: so to be wearing a crown in your dream tells of praise and rewards to come. Dreaming about a policeman's helmet

either personal or financial. Perhaps you need extra locks on the door, for example, or have you been thinking of taking out insurance or health cover lately? An alternative interpretation, since these items of clothing are coverups, lies in the implication of covering over, of hiding or disguising. Are there matters in your life that you wish were not brought to light? Or, if someone else is wearing a covering garment of any description, you need to question what he or she might be trying to hide.

Under wraps

Seeing yourself in a long coat might mean you are trying to hide the person underneath

implies that you will be dealing with matters connected with the law and authority, while a bowler hat might bring to mind financial or business affairs. If your hat is battered or lost, it may be a warning that you are in danger of damaging your reputation. If you dream that someone steals your hat, it could mean that someone in real life is trying to take your place.

TROUSERS

The expression "wearing the trousers" alludes to the boss of the household. Whoever, therefore, is wearing the trousers in your dream is taking the upper hand in a particular relationship.

OVERCOATS

Coats, raincoats and, for that matter, aprons and boilersuits, too, are garments that we wear to protect us, to keep us warm, or clean and tidy. To envelop yourself in a coat or to put on overalls hints at a need for protection,

UNDERWEAR

In erotic dreams, the focus of attention often centers on underwear, although the type, condition and color of these garments may be making a direct statement about your sex life. Lacy red lingerie, for example, may allude to passion and desire, whereas torn, discolored or unclean underclothes may suggest lost love, a decline in libido, or even feelings of guilt and dishonor.

Dressed to kill

Dramatic dressing in your dreams may imply a desire to seek attention

activity dreams

MOVEMENT AND TRAVEL

Any form of movement or travel in our dreams is a comment on the progress we are making in real life. Sometimes the dream will allude quite factually to a physical journey, perhaps replaying a recent trip or preparing us for an excursion in the future. At other times, a dream of this nature will be symbolic, describing our chosen "path" in life, and highlighting our current state of mind as we go about our daily business – whether we feel confident, for example, or unsure of ourselves, whether we have come upon obstacles to our plans or feel we are currently achieving our ambitions.

On quite a different level, dreams about travel may symbolize our spiritual journey, our inner development, and personal growth. The pleasures and pain we encounter in these dream journeys will reveal to us how well we are fulfilling our destinies and how successful we are being at bringing our talents and potential to fruition.

Pole position
Racing downhill could mean you are out of control

SETTING OUT ON A JOURNEY

Here is a dream about a new beginning. Setting off on a journey marks a new departure in our lives, a relocation, perhaps, or embarking on a new career. The anticipation in the dream, whether we are excited at the prospect or fear the coming changes, will be a reflection on how we feel in regard to the real life transition about to take place.

STREETS, ROADS, AND AVENUES

All pathways, whether they be narrow alleys or wide, tree-lined boulevards, set the scene around which your journey is taking place and reflect the ease or difficulties you are currently encountering in your life. A steep, tortuous ascent may suggest that you are having to put a good deal of effort into your work and relationships at present. Large boulders

strewn across your path imply obstacles that impede your progress – perhaps a colleague or member of your family is making life difficult for you in some way. Finding yourself in a cul-de-sac may highlight the fact that you are in a dead-end job and prompt you to apply for a more interesting position. Sauntering down a well-lit avenue implies that you have leisure time to enjoy; perhaps you have come to an end of a busy period in your life, or have just taken early retirement.

IN THE DRIVER'S SEAT

And how are you traveling? Are you walking, or riding a horse, or perhaps even cruising in a chauffeur-driven stretch limousine? Whichever method of transportation you are using continues the theme of your progress and shows how you are coping with the situations that arise. If you are walking, riding a bike, on horseback, or driving a vehicle of any kind, you are in charge and in control of your affairs, since being in the saddle, or in the driver's seat, means that you can make your own decisions as to where you are going. Being driven by somebody else has several interpretations. Might it be that you are at another person's bidding in your life at present, that you have no other choice right now but to go along with those around you? Sitting back and enjoying the ride may suggest that you are having an easy time of things. Being taken here and there may suggest that you are on a wild goose chase, or perhaps this dream is saying that you are simply being "taken for a ride."

MAPS

Dreaming that you are consulting a map may foretell that you will be traveling in the near future. If you are having trouble deciphering the route, it could mean that you are unsure of where life is taking you at present. The same is true if, in your dream, you find yourself in a foreign country and can neither recognize your surroundings nor understand those around you. This may well reflect that you are having problems relating to, or communicating with, people at home or at work.

Where do we go from here?
If you need to borrow a map, your dream is suggesting you seek advice

activity dreams

VEHICLES

Complications that arise when we are making travel arrangements in real life, delays on our journeys, or money worries that result from expensive trips, may mirror themselves in our dreams. These we can recognize as factual replays, discharging our anger and frustration through dreamtime traffic jams or dramatic car chases. Similarly, exciting holidays or relaxing breaks may also be reflected in pleasant reveries.

The type of transportation we use in our dreams will serve to elaborate futher on how we are dealing with our everyday lives. Whether we find ourselves traveling alone or in company, whether we are passengers or taking the helm, and, indeed, how we feel throughout the trip, will all give insights into the degree of control we have in our day-to-day affairs.

BUSES AND TRAINS

Passengers on buses and trains travel along a set route, so to dream that you are using one of these forms of public transport may be bringing to the fore that you are set in your ways, or that you need more variety in your daily life. Alternatively, this might be suggesting that you are following the crowd instead of thinking for yourself. To dream of missing the bus might mean that you are in danger of missing an important opportunity. And to get on the wrong train altogether warns that you may be taking the wrong decisions.

CARS

For many people cars are status symbols, and dreaming of owning a Lamborghini might simply be a wish-fulfillment dream. For men in particular, cars in dreams can symbolize their driving ambitions or their driving passions. For either sex, being in the driver's seat represents being in control of their lives, taking charge of their own destinies and steering their own fates. Loss of control of the dream car, of course, suggests a similar loss of control over events in your life. Happily cruising along the freeway implies a sense of liberation and a bid for independence. The condition of the car, too, will throw some light on the interpretation of the dream. A dirty or rusty car is an allusion to unused talents, or a prompt to improve one's image.

SEA VESSELS

Water in our dreams is associated with our emotions, so sailing in a boat is often a comment on how we are dealing with our

Driving ambition
Being in the driver's seat shows that you have taken charge of your life

feelings. A yacht gliding over calm waters implies that life is "plain sailing" at the moment. Being tossed about on rough seas warns of impending quarrels. Ships that navigate between rocks or through narrow channels tell you to "steer" clear of trouble or alert you to restrictions ahead. And if you dream that you are "paddling your own canoe," it may well be a reflection of your desire for independence. If you dream that your boat sinks, it may foreshadow the failure of your plans.

AIRCRAFT

Flying in dreams is associated with ambitions and aspirations. The higher we fly, the higher are our ideals. Being the pilot means taking power into our own hands, while being a passenger in the airplane suggests that our success is dependent on other people. A bumpy, turbulent flight indicates that our progress is not as smooth or as easy as we would like it to be.

BICYCLES, SKIS AND ROLLER SKATES

Any means of transport that is self-propelled, such as a bicycle, a skateboard or skis for example, shows that the road to success is very much in our own hands, but will depend on personal effort, just as pedaling requires physical exertion. Expressions such as "get your skates on" may be mirrored in images of putting on ice-skates, the implicit message being one of encouragement to work faster and more efficiently.

activity dreams

FLYING

Dreams about flying can take several forms, from free flight to traveling in an aircraft, from birds on the wing to a kite on a string. They are, perhaps, more common amongst youngsters than in adult dreamers but, at whatever age they occur, these can be some of the most exhilarating dreams of all.

INTO THE BLUE

A dream of free flight where you are soaring like a bird in the sky often follows an achievement in life. Passing your exams, perhaps, getting promotion or winning the lottery might prompt this type of dream. Essentially, it describes a feeling of confidence, success, and self-assurance. The message from your unconscious here is that in your waking life you have the power to overcome insuperable odds, to beat the opposition, and to triumph over adversity. Flying high into the sky also brings with it the notion of high ideals and aspirations – the higher you fly, the higher you have set your goals. If you are flying amidst fluffy, cotton-wool clouds, you should question whether you might not be too idealistic, and go through life with your "head in the clouds." More positive and reassuring is a dream in which you catch sight of the land below, because this suggests that while you may have grand ambitions, you still have a fix on reality, and therefore you are unlikely to get carried away with impractical schemes.

Up in the air
Are you flying too high, with your head in the clouds?

PLANE TRAVEL

It is not unusual for vacationers to dream of their chosen method of travel before setting off on their journeys, so those about to jet off to distant lands might well dream about flying in an aircraft. Airplanes, however, do symbolize escape, for they offer us the opportunity to be transported, within a mere matter of hours, far away from our normal work and routine lives. A dream in which you are the pilot of the plane suggests that

you have the power in your own hands to release yourself from burdens and worries. This is your subconsicous reminding you that you are in charge and in control of your own destiny and that you can make whatever decisions are necessary to improve your life. Being a passenger on a plane, though, may be suggesting that while there is the possibility of change, you may not be in control of the entire situation.

High flier
Piloting a craft indicates that you have the ability to escape your worries

BIRDS

To see a bird in flight in your dreams represents a desire for freedom. This might imply wanting to rise above restrictions, duties, or burdensome responsibilities. Or it could suggest the freedom that comes when we improve our standing and status in life.

The type of bird you see flying is significant, as the message may well be found in its associated characteristics. For example, an eagle represents power and, because of its keen eyesight, it also symbolizes insight. This suggests that your success depends on your vigilance, on your ability to read between the lines or capacity for looking inwards at your own strengths. A buzzard, on the other hand, may be advising you not to be quite so predatory as you chase after your goals. A rooster may hint at egotistical behavior. An owl encourages the use of wisdom. A stork brings news of new beginnings. And a robin foretells good fortune and success.

KITES

A kite is an interesting dream theme since it flies in the air, yet is linked to the ground by its string. If you are flying the kite in your dream it suggests you have high-flying ideas that are, nevertheless, practical and workable since the kite is essentially "grounded" and under your control. By all accounts, this would imply a winning formula.

activity dreams

CLIMBING

Dreams that contain images of climbing are fairly common, especially so amongst ambitious people. Dreams in which stairs are mounted or where peaks are scaled appear to comment on our hopes, dreams, and aspirations. Both the context and the events being depicted here will give us clues as to the progress we are making in the pursuit of our goals. Aside from materialistic progress, though, climbing dreams may also make a statement about our intellectual or spiritual journey through life. Freud, however, maintained that this type of dream had a more erotic connotation and he parallelled the ascent to the summit of a mountain with the climax in sexual coitus.

LADDERS

Just as we refer to climbing up the career ladder, so a ladder in a dream presents us with our attempts to improve our status in life. An easy climb reflects the confidence we have in our own abilities to succeed. But missing rungs represent the challenges we are likely to meet along the way. Slipping back down the ladder, of course, points to failures and missed opportunities.

SCALING MOUNTAINS

Because the peaks of a mountain reach up to the heavens, climbing mountains in dreams places the emphasis more on the spiritual development of the individual rather than on the success in worldly matters. Striving to reach the summit mirrors a desire to learn more, to reach higher, to gain greater understanding, and to master better skills. The tougher the climb, the more determination and personal endurance needs to be found. Life at present, the unconscious is pointing out, appears to be an "uphill struggle." Moreover, jagged edges, rocky outcrops, or boulders across the path that slow the ascent all warn of demanding situations in waking life that will test the dreamer's resourcefulness and inner resolve.

ESCALATORS AND ELEVATORS

Because escalators and elevators ascend to the top of a building and descend to the basement, they convey a similar message in dreams as stairs do, but with one notable difference – they take the hard work out of the climb! Dreams in which these mechanical devices are involved suggest success and achievement without much personal effort.

Uphill struggle

A difficult climb warns you of equally tough situations in life, which demand inner resolve

STAIRS

A flight of stairs and their condition will symbolize the ease or difficulty you are experiencing in achieving your ambitions in day-to-day life. Walking up a grand, carpeted staircase, for example, suggests you will reach your target with little difficulty. Treads that crumble underfoot, missing steps, or whole flights that have rotted away altogether represent problems and complications that stand in your way.

How you resolve the difficulties in order to arrive at the top will suggest the outcome of your endeavors. The steeper the stairs and the greater the effort required, the harder you will have to work to achieve your aims. Reaching the top and entering the attic symbolizes the development of intellectual understanding, and the exploration and growth of latent or emerging talents.

Conversely, climbing downstairs to the basement is a classic symbol that you are ready to confront your deepest fears. However, when walking down the stairs, tripping or stumbling are warnings of potential setbacks to your aims.

activity dreams

FALLING

Often frightening, particularly for young children, dreams about falling can be triggered by physiological factors, an aspect that should not be overlooked in the interpretation of this theme. On a different level, falling dreams may symbolize the sort of situation that the dreamer associates in their life with a "fall from grace." Very occasionally, however, dreaming about a fall can carry a definite element of warning in its imagery.

PHYSICAL EFFECTS

There is a common sleep phenomenon that most people are familiar with. You are tucked up in bed, warm, cozy and comfortable and, as your mind conjures thoughts of floating through a flowery meadow on a warm, sunny day, you slowly drift off to sleep. All of a sudden, you plunge headlong into a bottomless pit. Startled, you try to save your fall and in so doing you jolt yourself back to consciousness again. You realize you were dreaming. You relax some more and, for the second time, you drift off to sleep again, this time without incident.

This familiar reaction is known as a myoclonic spasm and is akin to hiccups and other types of involuntary twitches. It occurs because when we fall asleep our muscles relax and lose their tone in a kind of sleeping paralysis. Without muscle function we become perilously vulnerable so, even as we sleep, the sensation of losing our strength triggers our brains to send out alarm signals to immediately reactivate our muscles. And it is this sudden snapping back of muscle control that causes the jolt that wakes us up.

When it occurs, we normally experience the myoclonic jolt in the early part of our sleep, but there is reason to believe that another physical effect may come into play and cause these dreams. Researchers have found that sometimes as we sleep we experience a sudden drop in blood pressure and this, it is thought, can be responsible for inducing that sinking sensation that our unconscious weaves into a dramatic fall.

SYMBOLIC FALLS

On a symbolic level, dreams about falling are associated with insecurity, a lack of confidence or simply a fear of failure. High achievers, in particular, are prone to this type of dream. Being afraid of not making the grade, of failing to secure a position, of losing our grip at work or being unable to cope with the demands of our career, can all trigger a falling dream. So, too, can negative events such as losing one's job, the breakup of a relationship, or the loss of a quantity of money. From a moral point of view, making a mistake, breaking a promise, committing a shameful deed, loss of face or even of one's virginity may equally be represented by a fall in a dream.

WARNING SIGNS

Although rare, a dream in which you see yourself falling may actually be warning you of a potential accident, particularly so if you recognize the environment that is being portrayed. An example might be a fall from a balcony window that looks remarkably like your own. In this case, it might be quite possible that when awake you half-spotted a fault in one of the railings and unconsciously registered that as dangerous. Now, in your sleep, your unconscious brings that danger to your attention and plays out a scenario of what could happen if the damage is not repaired. If, in a falling dream, you recognize the setting, it is well worth a careful investigation of the site when you wake up.

Free fall

A sudden drop in blood pressure can trigger a dramatic plunge in your dream

activity dreams

RUNNING

There are many different ways in which our unconscious minds bring our innermost fears to the fore in our dreams. One of these is by presenting us with images of pursuit. Dreams about being chased are often frightening, so by rights they fall into the category of nightmares. But, however they may be categorized, these are classic anxiety dreams. Chasing after someone, or something, is quite another matter and carries a different message altogether. Running in a race or running purely for the exhilaration add yet more facets to this theme. The emotions that accompany a dream about running will instantly pinpoint the nature of the dream and will throw light upon its level of interpretation.

RUNNING AWAY

We dream of running away when the pressures in our daily lives become intolerable. There may be a thousand and one reasons why we seek to escape from our daily burdens – financial commitments, emotional responsibilities, job deadlines, and all the other day-to-day worries that put a strain on our physical and mental resources. Under these circumstances, a dream of running away may be simply wish-fulfillment, and the prevailing emotional response is one of relief. Alternatively, though, this dream may be offering timely advice, alerting us that a break from the stressful routine is now essential to our well-being.

BEING CHASED

Not all dreams of running away feature a pursuer. Those that do are categorized as dreams of being chased. These are the dreams that we find highly distressing and that leave us panting for breath and with a pounding heart. Sometimes, as in the case of a school bully or a dangerous local dog, we recognize our pursuer, or at least we can sense who (or what) he or she is, which makes the source of

Run for your life
Dreams of running away express a desire for freedom or escape from responsibilities

our fears quite plain. At other times, the pursuer may be a wild animal, a dark entity, or we may have just a vague feeling of terror, so identifying the root of our anxiety may not be so easy. Perhaps the dream pursuer is presented in a different guise, taking the salient characteristics, if not the actual form, of whatever is causing our fear. For example, a menacing shadow in the dream may represent a stalker in real life. Psychologists advise that if you experience dreams of being chased (and especially if these are recurrent), you should try to reenter the dream and turn to face your opponent. It is even better if you can manage to shout at your pursuer, throw stones at it, or drive it away. Facing the fear in the dream, it is believed, will help you to build up the courage to confront and overcome that anxiety in waking life.

Turning point

Don't run from your fear: face your demons and you will gradually build up your courage in waking life

IN HOT PURSUIT

Dreams in which you are the pursuer may be broken down into two types. Either you are angry with someone and are chasing that person to get even, or you are chasing an ambition, a desire, or a goal. The first will engender feelings of aggression, while the second will leave you longing for satisfaction.

RACING

Running simply for the joy of it in a dream can bring an immense sense of freedom and release. But running a race against other people symbolizes the competition you are experiencing in your conscious state. You might have this dream before an exam or a job interview, for example, or perhaps if you are in competition with a rival for the affection of a potential lover.

pain and pleasure

PHYSICAL SENSATIONS

Part of the mechanics of sleeping and dreaming requires our muscles to go into a state of deep relaxation. One reason for this might be that loss of muscle tone is a necessary precaution in case we find ourselves so aroused by the contents of our dreams that we physically act them out. It is this near paralysis of our limbs that may explain why, in some dreams, our legs feel as if they are filled with lead.

Other physiological factors, such as lowering of body temperature or of blood pressure, may trigger dream sensations like those of drowning or sinking in quicksand. Nevertheless, whatever might be responsible for producing these physical sensations, their symbolic meanings are no less fascinating when we experience them in our dreams.

HEAVY LIMBS

To dream that your legs are so heavy that, no matter how hard you try to run away you simply cannot make any headway, may be implying that you would like to escape from a burdensome situation in your waking life but you are unable to do so because you are tied down by responsibilities. Or perhaps you are trying to get away from a relationship or an influence that you know has a detrimental effect upon you, yet something is preventing you from making a clean break. Alternatively, could it be that you have not made the sort of progress in your career that you would have liked? If this is the case, perhaps your dream is telling you that you are dragging your heels and that with a little more effort on your part, you could achieve your goal.

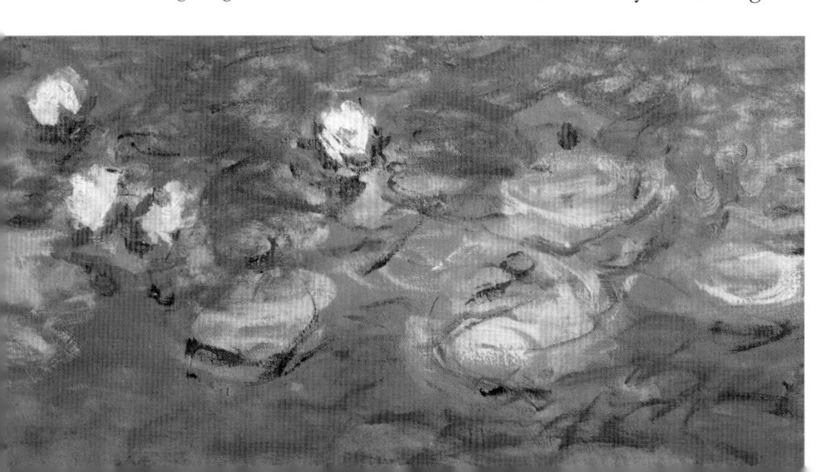

Depth gauge
Drowning or being out of your depth shows life's demands are getting too much

FEELING TRAPPED

Dreams of being trapped symbolize restrictions and constraints in real life. What are your restraints? If the ceiling has caved in on top of you, for example, it may represent the weight of responsibility, or the emotional or financial pressures that you are struggling against. Being imprisoned or locked in a room in your dream may reflect a curtailment of your personal freedom, perhaps because at this point in your life you are compelled to follow other people's rules or comply with their wishes. Being locked in a cellar, though, may symbolize that your own inhibitions prevent you from making better progress in your life. In dreams, entrapment of any sort often reflects personal frustrations, helplessness, and a loss of control.

the cause of our daily distresses. An office manager, for example, struggling to meet deadlines or overwhelmed by a massive workload, may dream that he or she is drowning beneath a sea of paper. Suffocating is a variation on this theme, symbolizing a difficulty in coping with life. And if you try to

DROWNING

A very common dream theme, drowning, suggests that somehow we are out of our depth or that we are finding it hard to cope with the demands our lives or careers are making on us. For instance, getting in too deep emotionally may be reflected by the sensation of being engulfed by tidal waves. However, we may not always drown in water, for the medium into which we sink can give some obvious clues to

scream but make no sound it implies that your cries for help are either not being heard, or are going unanswered.

CHOKING

If you have said something for which you feel guilty, or which is about to rebound on you, you may dream that you are choking. It may be that the words are sticking in your throat, and you are choking on them.

Proud moment
Choking in your dreams may show that you are having to "swallow your pride"

pain and pleasure

FOOD AND DRINK

Nourishment is the primary purpose of food, and it is essential to our survival. But food indicates much more than simple nutrition, and the subject as a whole needs to be viewed on a much broader canvas. Depending on your circumstances at the time of the dream, preparing, cooking, serving, eating, or drinking may have implications of a physical, spiritual, intellectual, social, or even erotic nature.

PREPARING FOOD

The preparation of food for other people to eat is associated with a nurturing, supporting instinct. Perhaps you have lots of love to give. Or, if you are cooking in your dream, it may signify that you are "cooking up" a new scheme or a special plan. The same might apply if you are making tea or coffee in the sense that you are "brewing up" an idea.

EATING AND DRINKING

Going to bed hungry often prompts compensatory dreams of food, while a salty snack before bed might induce thirst and therefore

Apple of temptation
Images of juicy fruits represent both the erogenous zones and the whole subject of fertility

dreams of quenching drinks. To dream that you are hungry, however, may be interpreted as a desire, or a "hunger," for something in daily life. What are you hungry for? Power, knowledge, or love, perhaps. The symbolism behind the food you eat to satisfy that hunger will relate to those waking desires. Bread, for example, a colloquial term for cash, might suggest that you want money. Soft, ripe, juicy fruit, such as peaches and plums, has an altogether more sensual connotation.

Whether you are eating in company or alone, and whether the food is enjoyable or unpalatable, will all be highly significant to the meaning of this dream. The biblical sense of "breaking bread together," or of sharing a meal with friends and loved ones can reflect that you feel supported and contented with your domestic and social life. Eating alone may mirror your own solitude or loneliness, or your feelings of being unloved. Puddings and other soft food can imply a need for comfort. Being forced to eat a bitter or unpalatable dish may highlight difficulties, or a sense of disgust over a particular situation, or even a need to eat "humble pie." Spilled drinks or spoiled, moldy food can point to a waste of time, to disappointments and lost opportunities.

TYPES OF FOOD

Over time, certain foods have developed particular associations. The rounded, fleshy, lusciousness of fruit, for example, can bring to mind breasts, bottoms, and the sexual organs in both real life and in our dreams. But, as in the expression "fruit of one's loins," they may also represent fertility. Eggs, too, are symbols of fertility and new life. Cream, as in *crème de la crème* may imply excellence, the tops, the best. Chocolate and luxury go together, bringing indulgence to mind. Confectionery and sweetmeats suggest rewards, "taking the cake" implying the winner. Bitter lemons or sour food, on the other hand, may reflect harsh experiences, unpleasant duties, broken promises, or emotional disappointments. Drinking champagne, though, foretells celebration and success. The green of a vegetable can signify vitality, but if the image is of a limp lettuce, this may be bringing to your attention the fact that you are tired and exhausted. And showing you a sack of potatoes may be a device that your unconscious employs to get you to exercise more, lest you turn into a "couch potato!"

Consuming desire
The food you dream of will indicate what you are "hungry" for in life

DIETING

Restrictions, cutting down, or going without are all facets of dieting, and though we normally associate this with food intake, a dream about dieting may actually be referring to other areas of our lives. Cutting down on waste for example, limiting social engagements, or taking on fewer work commitments may equally apply here.

pain and pleasure

SUCCESS AND FAILURE

We all need an occasional pat on the back as an acknowledgment of our efforts and as a boost to our self-confidence. But our successes are not always recognized, and, though of remarkable personal significance, our private triumphs may not always attract the plaudits from others that they justly merit. However, whether or not the world openly hails us for our achievements, we can be sure that our unconscious minds will not miss an opportunity to give credit where credit is due. Very often our dreams will celebrate our accomplishments and give us the glory that our deeds deserve.

Failure, or rather our fear of failure, anxieties about personal worthlessness in our lives or of an inability to fulfill other people's expectations are also conditions that are commented on by the unconscious in our dreams. Sometimes these dreams of catastrophe and disappointment hark back to real events when our hopes were dashed. More often, they bring to the surface our own hidden feelings of inadequacy or low self-esteem.

DREAMS OF ACHIEVEMENT

In dreams, mountaintops symbolize the pinnacle of success, so to see yourself sitting comfortably on the topmost peak, especially when the image is accompanied by a sense of exhilaration, marks the culmination of your achievements. Offerings of jewels, of crowns, or of laurel wreaths, too, represent tributes to your endeavors. Think of the expression, "crowning glory" if these are placed on your head. Other dreams that pay tribute to your success, or that presage success to come, might involve seeing yourself come first in a race, blowing your own trumpet, holding a trophy, waving a flag, being awarded a medal, or being applauded by a crowd.

DREAMS OF FAILURE

Examinations, auditions, or interviews commonly feature in dreams associated with

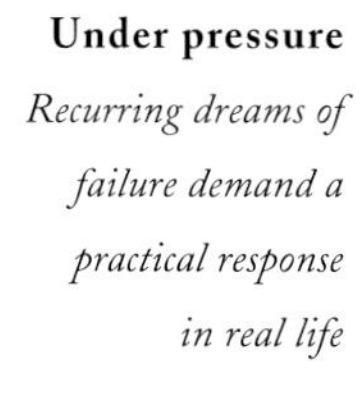

Under pressure
Recurring dreams of failure demand a practical response in real life

failure. The classical scenario here might depict you sitting at an exam desk, turning over the question sheet and discovering, to your dismay, that you cannot answer a single question. Or perhaps the paper is written in a language you cannot understand. A similar dream might include an audition where, put on the spot, you find yourself lost for words or you completely forget the piece you had prepared to recite. Or you may be talking to an interview panel but they misunderstand what you say or, worse, you hear yourself saying all the wrong things. Being late, missing your cue, or being delayed so that the train or the bus leaves without you is an alternative on this theme.

Over the moon

If our successes are not acknowledged in life, we may dream of glory

People experience this type of dream, which exposes some sort of incompetence, at times when they feel their lives are out of their control. Perhaps they are under work pressures or perhaps, in wanting to please others, they take too much upon themselves, before realizing they have overcommitted their time and energies. Through recurring dreams of failure our unconscious tells us that it is time to reassess our attitudes and priorities and take practical measures to build up our confidence and destress our lives.

pain and pleasure

EMBARRASSMENT

Whether due to a mistake of our own making, or because of other people's maliciousness, few of us relish being laughed at or being made to look foolish. Finding ourselves in an embarrassing situation is just as mortifying in our dreams as it is in our waking lives. Dreams in which we feel uncomfortable, distressed, or ill-at-ease often point to our vulnerabilities and fear of being found inadequate.

NUDITY

Some of the most common embarrassment dreams involve nudity. You might, for example, dream that you are standing at the checkout in the middle of a busy supermarket, when you suddenly notice, to your horror, that you are completely naked. This type of dream may recur in different variations at particular times in your life: if you are under stress, if you have taken on more work than you can reasonably handle, or if you have been asked to perform a task at which you think you lack expertise. Essentially, the embarrassment of finding yourself naked in a public place where everybody is staring at you reveals a fear of psychological exposure. This is pointing to your worries that you will in some way be found wanting, that others will see through your pretences or judge you to be incompetent.

Another variation might be a dream in which you are taking your clothes off in public. Here, the fear is of disclosure, an anxiety that you might in some way drop your guard or possibly reveal your true self, especially if there is any aspect of your character or background

that you wish to keep hidden. This may well be a warning from your unconscious that you are giving away too many personal secrets and therefore making yourself vulnerable. To see a person you are familiar with taking off his or her clothes in front of you may be a wish-fulfillment dream. On the other hand, this could suggest that you are beginning to see through his or her façade to the real person beneath. Of course, feelings of shame about personal nudity may simply be highlighting inhibitions. Conversely, feelings of exhilaration from being naked in public may suggest either spiritual innocence or a flamboyant nature.

Awkward moments
Above: Saying the wrong thing, at the wrong time, to the wrong person...

Don't look now
Left: Finding yourself out in the open with no protection is very disturbing psychologically

INAPPROPRIATE CLOTHES

Dreaming that you arrive at a function inappropriately dressed may reflect an actual event, or it might represent an incident in your waking hours in which you inadvertently committed a *faux pas*. Symbolically, this theme describes a fear of making a mistake or showing oneself up in public, and consequently being subjected to ridicule.

COMPROMISING SITUATIONS

A fear of depersonalization, a dread of public humiliation, or anxieties concerning loss of respect underlie dreams in which you are discovered in compromising situations. A classic example is dreaming that you are sitting on a toilet in full view of everyone walking past. A similar theme for a married person might include being found *in flagrante delicto* with someone other than the dreamer's spouse.

the natural world

THE SEASONS

The short, sunless days of winter have a profound effect on our moods, lowering our spirits and inducing depression. In contrast, the brighter, lengthening days of spring, with their promise of growth and new life, fill us with inspiration and hope for the future. Each season influences us in its own way, shaping and conditioning our affairs, and leaving its own mark on our lives as we progress through the year.

In precisely the same way, images of the seasons will affect our dreams, putting a subtle but distinctive stamp on the drama that is being unfolded by our sleeping minds. Whether as a backdrop to the main action, or actually taking the starring role themselves, seasons will give clues to help you decipher the message of your dream.

SPRING

Elements of spring in a dream might manifest themselves as green shoots emerging from the earth, or buds unfolding their tender leaves, as a nest of newly-laid eggs, or as lambs gamboling in a field. Spring brings with it rebirth, an exchange of the old for the new, fresh hopes and new beginnings. So a dream containing elements of spring foreshadows a new phase in your life. It is preparing you for the next stage and encouraging you to go forward with hope and expectation.

Notice, too, whether the dreams you have in springtime carry different messages from those you experience at other times of the year. For, as the warmth of the earth is rekindled and the sap begins to rise, so our attention, whether we are awake or asleep, turns to thoughts of the future, to new avenues and different directions – all of which will affect the contents of our dreams at this time of year.

SUMMER

The sweet scent of roses, blue cornflowers, and red poppies among the ripening wheat, cotton-wool clouds scudding across an azure

Sunny skies
Prophetic and imaginative dreams are more likely to occur during the summer months

sky, picnics in the countryside, and long, hot, lazy days are traditional images associated with summertime. Whenever scenes that remind you of summer appear in your dreams, the message is distinctly joyous, foretelling contentment and happiness ahead. Or, if you have been working hard, this dream will remind you that it is time to take things easy, take a short break, or plan your vacation.

Dreams that occur in the summer months are said to contain information that is more imaginative and original than at other times of the year. Many are also prophetic.

FALL

In fall, Mother Nature paints the land with colors of red, copper, and burnished gold.

Branches are heavy with fruit, grapes bloom on the vine and in the fields the farmers cut the ripened corn. Everywhere the harvest is in full swing, while the crunch of fallen leaves underfoot and early morning mists hint at cooler weather. When the colors and sounds of fall permeate your dreams, think of fruition and completion. These dreams will foretell rewards that may be reaped from past efforts and hard work.

A dream in which crops are destroyed, however, warns of broken promises, or it might suggest that a plan in the pipeline fails to come up to your expectations.

WINTER

Icicles glistening on a frosty day with the tracery of branches against a leaden sky; figures skating on a pond; the excited squeals of children, encased in hats and mittens, as they race down slowclad slopes on their sleds and makeshift toboggans: these are all scenes that bring wintertime to mind. As the weather turns colder we draw inside our houses and, huddled around the hearth, we see pictures in the fire. This withdrawing inside is implicit in the message of dreams that depict images of winter. For these dreams suggest inner journeys, spiritual exploration, and a time for personal reflection.

Like the plants that conserve their energies deep inside the earth, dreams in wintertime, or those that feature winter scenery, tell of inner strengths, of contemplation, of harnessing power, and biding one's time. Now is not the time for bold new moves, these dreams tell us. Now is the time to reflect, to consolidate, to harbor the seeds that promise, next season, to bring forth new life.

Golden leaves

Fall colors in dreams mirror the successful outcome of your plans and projects

the natural world

THE WEATHER

With phrases such as "it's raining in my heart" or "you are my sunshine," skillful songwriters use weather metaphors to convey mood and emotion. In just the same way, your subconscious uses a similar play on words involving the climate to describe your hidden feelings or to set the scene in your dreams.

SUNSHINE

Just about everyone feels better when the sun shines, and if the sun is shining in your dream, you can be sure the message is a positive one. This is a sign of creative expression, and sunny scenes reflect feelings of happiness and well-being. Think of a breakthrough in your waking life if the sun breaks through a cloud in your dream. If, for example, you have been going through difficulties, or have had a quarrel with your partner, the image of the sun coming out from behind a cloud is a reassurance that you will find a solution or patch things up very soon.

RAINBOW

A symbol of hope and success for the future, a rainbow is a glorious image in a dream. Remember, too, that colors are significant, so the meaning of any color that is emphasized should also be taken into consideration when you are interpreting your dream.

RAIN

In dreams, as in real life, heavy rain can put a dampener on things. But rain also has a positive side, for it washes clean, freshens the air and is essential for the greening of the land. So, depending on your circumstances and the rest of the action in the dream, rain can, on the one hand, be describing the lowering of your mood, or the spoiling of plans. On the other, it may be denoting a cleansing away of your fears and doubts, clearing your thoughts in order to make room for fresh new ideas and inspiration.

CLOUDS

Heavy, gray clouds can throw a shadow over proceedings and in dreams they may be warning that problems or complications are brewing. A ray of sunshine or the hint of a silver lining will improve the outlook considerably. Flying or floating among the clouds is associated with high aspirations, ambitious ideas, and success.

STORMY WEATHER

Hurricanes or violent wind suggests a force in waking which is beyond our control. It can represent passion, and being swept helplessly along indicates that we do not have the power

to resist our heart's desires or the advances of a suitor. Spiritually, dreaming of wind could signify the intensity of belief, just as the Holy Spirit was represented by wind in the Bible. Additionally, to dream of a tornado does not signify destruction but cleansing. Devastating all that stands in its path, the tornado removes obstructions and clears a new path forward, creating potential for new life – the calm after the storm.

LIGHTNING

Flashes of lightning are synonymous with flashes of inspiration. Let this encourage you to act on any brilliant ideas you may have over the next day or so. When thunder accompanies the lightning, though, it brings in the mighty forces of nature that are outside our control. Here, then, might be timely advice to think carefully about the consequences of your actions before taking any decisions that might prove irrevocable.

MIST AND FOG

Because mist and fog obscure the vision in dreams, these warn of confusion and an inability to see the whole picture.

ICE AND SNOW

Have you made a mistake or slipped up recently? If so, a vision of slippery ice may be bringing this to your attention. Ice and snow are cold – perhaps someone is giving you the cold shoulder. Or, because these are forms of frozen water, this dream may describe cool emotions and a lack of affection.

Rainy days

A violent downpour or storm depicts emotional upsets or warns of conflict ahead

the natural world

LANDSCAPE

Like a stage play, the drama of a dream is usually set against a backdrop. As you dream, try to notice whether this background scenery is composed of an idyllic rural tableau filled with flowers and butterflies, or of a barren, rocky wasteland, as it has a central role to play in the message of the dream. Moreover, it is often here that we can find valuable information that will yield clues to the outcome of any decisions we are about to take in our everyday lives.

GARDENS, FIELDS, AND PARKLANDS

Green parks, leafy trees, colorful flowers, and lush plants are all excellent omens confirming that we are coping well in our lives, that we have an optimistic outlook, and that we feel spiritually, mentally, and emotionally fulfilled. To glimpse a distant green garden, field, or parkland in an otherwise barren setting promises better times in store once your current problems are over. However, bare trees, faded blooms, or devasted crops warn that difficulties or restrictions may lie ahead.

HILLS AND MOUNTAINS

Viewing high land from a distance suggests unfulfilled ambitions. The pervading mood in the dream, such as determination, excitement, or regret, will reveal whether or not the dreamer will reach his or her goals. Gently rolling hills suggest the tasks ahead are comparatively easy, while craggy mountains may imply that challenges should be expected.

Bridge the gap
Above: To dream of a bridge may be an indication that help is on its way

Earthly paradise
Left: A lush, tropical landscape reflects optimism and overall fulfillment in life

Climbing a mountain is also associated with ambition. Sitting on top of a hill and viewing the lush countryside around symbolizes success.

SEASCAPES, RIVERS, AND CAVES

Water in our dreams represents our emotions, so any action that takes place in or around the river or the sea will have a bearing on our current feelings and relationships. Sunbathing, or generally having fun on the beach, suggests you are relaxed and having a pleasant time in your love life at the moment. Walking along a deserted beach, though, may imply that you are lonely. If the river is flowing smoothly or the sea is calm, you are emotionally in control, but if the water is in any way agitated, it points to turbulent emotions. Caves in the cliff walls make fascinating dream themes with several possible interpretations, since they may denote the dark, unexplored recesses of the mind, or undeveloped talents and potential, or, as a symbol of the vagina, they can represent the female sexual organs. Entering a cave may reflect the growth of personal understanding, the beginnings of spiritual development, or the act of sexual union.

URBAN SETTINGS

If you recognize the neighborhood, the dream may be giving a factual comment on your day-to-day existence. An unfamiliar environment suggests either uncertainty or the start of new experiences. Beautiful architecture may be reminding you of a need for organization in your life. Well-lit areas imply you can see the way ahead, though dark streets may hint that the outcome of your actions is as yet unknown.

CROSSROADS AND BRIDGES

As in real life, arriving at a crossroads in your dream means that you have decisions to make. Bridges may symbolize strategies or helpful people that come to your assistance.

the natural world

ANIMALS

Animal dreams can be grouped into separate categories, because images of favorite pets are likely to carry quite a different message from, say, a dream about a ferocious tiger, or an infestation of ants. In our dreams, animals can represent our natural or primitive instincts. Or, in an abstract way, they may stand for the characteristics that we associate with individual creatures – the playfulness of a puppy, the long memory of the elephant, or the regal bearing of the lion. Sometimes, too, people we know in waking life may be represented by specific animals in our dreams, purely because we recognize in them similar qualities. A pretty niece may be represented by a fluffy kitten, but a spiteful colleague by a spitting, sharp-clawed cat; a mischievous son by a monkey, but a well-built, menacing neighbor by a gorilla.

When dealing with animal symbolism, however, it is as well to bear in mind that not all cultures share the same opinions of particular animals' character. The Chinese, for example, see the rat not as a spineless coward but as a shrewd and resourceful creature. And, according to the Native American tradition, wild animals who might in other cultures be considered threatening become powerful spirit guides.

PETS

A pet animal may, of course, appear in a factual dream as itself, helping to set the scene of the action. It may symbolize coziness, security, contentment or protection. A pet may stand in for a person we know – a dog for a best friend, perhaps, since dogs are also known as "man's best friend." Many people who have lost a beloved pet report seeing it in their dreams as if returning to reassure its owner that all is well or that it is, albeit in spirit, still keeping a watchful eye on the household. And this, as well as the Native American's spirit guide, accords with ancient dream books that tell of animals appearing in our dreams in the form of messengers or guardians. It is important, then, to take note of whatever message the animal brings.

FARMYARD ANIMALS

If a farmyard animal features prominently in your dreams, considering its associated characteristics will help in the interpretation. Hens, for example, fuss and cluck over their chicks. Is the message perhaps that you might be a little domineering. If you tend to go along with other people rather than think for yourself, perhaps you might see a flock of sheep in your dreams. Riding a horse, though, implies that you are firmly "in the saddle."

WILD ANIMALS

Often a component of nightmares, ferocious creatures such as lions or tigers all too often symbolize our waking fears. For example, an aggressive husband may be represented in a dream by a grizzly bear, or the worry of paying back a large financial debt may manifest itself in the form of a savage wolf trailing the dreamer's scent. Fearing a wild animal but finding that it is tame is a device used by the unconscious to show that the anxiety is groundless, or that the problem can be worked out with less difficulty than expected. A caged animal may suggest that your fear is being contained, or perhaps repressed. But always consider the symbolism attached to a wild animal, for the message of the dream may lie in its associated characteristics. One of these creatures may be representing you or someone you know in your life.

WINGED CREATURES

Dreams of flying are associated with ambition, so to see an eagle soaring in the sky suggests that you have high ideals. Doves are traditional emblems of peace, so one may appear in your dreams after quarrels or disputes with the people you love. Bees, on the other hand, are a hive of industry, perhaps a hint that greater concentration at work will bring results. Butterflies may represent a superficial mentality but they can also symbolize transformation from one phase of your life to another.

INSECTS

Insects and irritation go together. Dreams featuring these creatures might occur if there are petty issues at work that need to be addressed, or fine detail, that requires your attention. Ants, however, may remind you that hard work and effort are required to achieve your goals.

Quiet life

Seeing a cow in your dream may imply that you are too docile

FISH

Because they swim in water, fish in our dreams are associated with our emotions. Alternatively, if they swim out of the depths they may symbolize talents or aspects of ourselves that are now coming to light.

universal symbols

THE ELEMENTS

Since the Middle Ages, the four elements – earth, air, fire, and water – have been recognized not only as quintessential components of the universe, but also as symbols that encapsulate the characteristics and qualities of all living things.

EARTH

Common sense, practicality, and hard work are associated with the earth. Dreaming that you are touching the earth or sitting on the ground is a message that you need to work things out logically. Essentially, this is saying "come down to earth," or "be realistic." Look at what is going on in your life rationally and try to find simple, practical solutions to your problems.

But the earth is also linked to fertility and creation, so to dream of a plowed field ready for planting suggests that this is a good time to sow the seeds of your ideas, and to lay your plans for the future. Mud is also part of the earth element. It is sticky and cloying, and to dream of this suggests you are getting bogged down, or "stuck in the mud." The message here, then, is to offload if you are overworked, or to take up new interests if your life has grown dull. Rocks, another aspect of this element, have a twofold meaning. They can represent stability or, when boulders block your path, they warn of obstacles ahead and difficult situations that will test your determination to the full.

AIR

Communications, intellectual pursuits and the world of ideas are associated with the air element which, in our dreams, may be symbolized by cool breezes rustling the leaves, seeing ourselves borne by the wind, or floating on a cloud. These gentle images bring to mind

creative thought processes, and the dream confirms that our ideas are both flowing and stimulating. When there is more turbulence, however, such as with hurricanes or tornadoes, then the dream is perhaps a warning that we are getting carried away with our ideas, that what we plan could get quite out of hand or might even be dangerous. If you dream that your head is in the clouds, it is a hint that you are being impractical. And if you, or a balloon, is floating back down to earth, your unconscious is telling you it is time to get your feet back on the ground and get to grips with reality.

FIRE

The context of the dream and of situations in your daily life will tell you whether a dream about fire has a positive or negative meaning. On the positive side, fire is warm and life-giving. As a beacon it gives light and, in combination with water, it can produce steam, which may be harnessed to give energy. Negatively, though, fire can destroy. It can flare spontaneously, then burn out of control, consuming everything in its path and leaving only ashes as proof of its passing. In our dreams, then, fire can represent the coziness of one's hearth and home. In the form of a candle it can suggest the throwing of light on to a problem. But fire also symbolizes passion – both love and hate. So to see a house on fire could mean you are either passionately in love or furious with rage. A fire that is out of control in your dreams is telling you that your feelings are out of control. If you see a fire engine, it means you have found a way of handling your emotions.

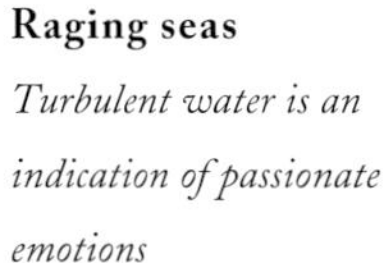

Raging seas
Turbulent water is an indication of passionate emotions

WATER

In dreams, water is a powerful symbol because it represents two fundamental areas of the dreamer's personality: the emotions and the unconscious self. We dream of water in so many different guises – sometimes as rain, as bath water, or as a stream. It may be clear or muddied, calm or turbulent, shallow or deep, all of which give clues to our emotional state at the time of the dream. A still lake reflects inner calm, and being swept away by a storm suggests emotions that are out of our control. The clearer the water, the greater the insight, but when murky, water suggests complications and an inability to penetrate the truth. The shallower the waters, the shallower the feelings. A sensation of drowning implies that you are somehow out of your depth, perhaps emotionally, or you may be inundated with responsibilities. But diving into deep waters means that you are beginning to explore the depths of your inner self.

universal symbols

SUN AND MOON

With city lights and buildings that mask the brilliance of the sky, it is not surprising that dreams about the heavenly bodies are perhaps not as common as they used to be. And yet, dreams featuring the sun and the moon release ancestral memories, link us with the collective unconscious, and bring to the forefront archetypal concepts that are fundamental to our existence. Here are images that awaken the imagination, that trigger intuition, and tap the deepest recesses of the sleeping mind. Moon and sun, female and male, night and day, disparate yet complementary forces that are together, quintessential to life.

THE SUN

A symbol of positive energy and yang in essence, the sun represents the masculine principle. Physically the source of light, it also stands for the light of understanding, for reason and logic, for power and strength. It is associated with higher consciousness, with self-awareness, with intelligence and the intellectual processes of the mind. To see the sun rising in your dreams means that hope will be rekindled. The same applies to the sun's rays, especially when they are seen to shine through the clouds. But a cloud passing in front of the sun, blocking out its light, suggests that your emotions could be clouding your judgment.

A beautiful sunset shows that although a part of our lives is coming to a close, there will be no upset at its passing, but we will be left with a feeling of completion and satisfaction. In addition, sunrise, noon when the sun is directly overhead, and sunset may mark the different stages of our lives: birth, maturity, and old age. Otherwise, if you are involved in an important project, these might represent the stages of its development, from inception through to completion.

Yin and yang
Right: The masculine force of the sun is complemented by the feminine principle of the moon

The closing day
Left: A beautiful sunset means you are content to let a phase of your life end

THE MOON

The moon is yin to the sun's yang. She represents the feminine principle – fertility, sensitivity, intuition, and introspection. She is the archetypal symbol of motherhood, and is regarded as creative, fecund, and nurturing. Just as the moon controls the tides, so she governs moods and feelings in our waking lives, and in our dreams she symbolizes our emotions and our inner selves by her various shapes and phases through her cyclical journey around the sun.

In your dream the moon may represent your own mother, female relatives or other female colleagues, yourself if you are a woman, or the anima or feminine side of your nature if you are a man. The action in your dream will pick up on an event that has occurred or make a comment about your relationship with those people.

To dream of the new moon foretells new beginnings, the start of a creative phase, while a full moon implies the culmination of your efforts. An eclipse, or a moon covered by clouds, hints at upsets or a problem looming on the horizon. A dream of a blood red moon was often thought of as presaging war or death.

Another facet of the moon is her link with the menstrual cycle and, interestingly, dream researchers have found that many women dream about the moon a day or so before they menstruate – perhaps a timely memo straight from the unconscious. Even more curious is the moon's association with fertility. Quite often, it seems, women who have recently conceived dream about the moon even before they themselves are consciously aware they are pregnant. Proof indeed that the unconscious does not miss a trick!

universal symbols

LIGHT AND DARKNESS

Light and dark, or sunshine and shadow, are powerful dream symbols of knowledge versus ignorance, of clarity as opposed to confusion, of intuitive insights in contrast to blind delusions. Light brings out what has been hidden: darkness hides the truth. In our dreams, pursuing the light leads to revelation and to conscious awareness.

CANDLE

Even the small flame of a candle is enough to illuminate the darkness, so to dream that you are lighting a candle means that you are throwing light on a situation, perhaps finding the answer to a problem in real life. Whatever the light reveals will hold the clue to the solution you seek. If the candle is blown out by the wind, there may be a setback to your progress or a disappointment in store. But if you blow out the candle yourself, it suggests that you are actively extinguishing or putting an end to a situation (or to a relationship, perhaps) in your life.

Ray of hope
A candle's flame throws light on a situation, perhaps helping you to solve problems

BEACONS

To see a beacon of light in the distance on a dark night inspires hope, and that is precisely the message the unconscious is conveying when a beacon appears in a dream. But beacons not only light up the darkness, they also show the way around obstacles and dangers. So here in your dream is a direction marker that will reveal the nature of the path that lies ahead of you.

ELECTRIC LIGHT

Cartoonists sometimes draw a lightbulb above a character's head to denote a sudden thought or a bright idea. In the same way, a light turned on in a dream implies just that – you will have a flash of inspiration or arrive at a profound insight. This is most encouraging if, in your waking hours, you are involved in any sort of creative or inventive work. If you dream that you are in a dark tunnel and you see light shining up ahead, you can be sure that your difficulties will soon be over. Opening a door and walking into a room that is ablaze with light symbolizes the beginning of a new phase in your life, and one that will be a great improvement on the present. If the light in your dream is noticeably dim, it suggests that the time is not yet right for you to put your ideas into action. There is potential there, but it requires more thought and more growth before you can bring your plans to fruition. Interestingly, if in your dream you attempt to turn on a light switch it is a signal from your unconscious, offering you the possibility to trigger a lucid dream. More information on these fascinating dreams, which may be used therapeutically, can be found on pages 32–33.

CURTAINS

To throw back the curtains and allow the sunlight to stream in through the window symbolizes your readiness to discover the truth about a certain situation in your life. Basically, you want to know more, to find out, to see further. Apart from the light – the new dawning, the realization – the view out of the window may give you more clues about what you can expect to find. Conversely, of course, to close the curtains means that you want to blank something out. Perhaps there is a situation that you wish not to confront, and in screening off the light, you are effectively drawing a veil over the matter.

ILLUMINATED FIGURES

As well as knowledge and conscious awareness, light is also used metaphorically in a religious sense. Christ, for example, is described as the "light of the world." In paintings, too, saints and holy men and women are depicted with haloes of light, a golden aura that radiates out and around their bodies. In a dream, a figure illuminated in this way may represent wisdom or spiritual enlightenment. Listen carefully if the figure speaks or offers you a gift, as this will impart guidance, inner strength, and understanding to help you in your daily life. Depending on the context of your dream, to move towards a shining light may be symbolic of inner spiritual growth.

Into the light
Moving from the darkness toward a light might suggest that a time for action is near

universal symbols

TIME

Before scientific research into dreams took place, it was believed that our dreams occurred in flashes, all the actions and images passing through our minds in a mere instant. However, the advent of sleep laboratories and the subsequent psychological observations on sleep patterns have fundamentally changed our understanding of the duration of a dream. By timing the rapid eye movement of a person who is asleep – the sign that the sleeper is "watching" a dream – researchers have established that dreams last as long as they take for the action to unfold before our eyes. In short, the duration of a dream approximates to real time.

However, the dream may condense time, skip over irrelevant parts, or combine incidents that took place in quite different historical periods, and may distort the sequence of events altogether.

In a dream, symbols or objects that measure time are no less interesting, and while dreams may have poetic licence to warp time and events, the unconscious maintains a firm grasp on the here and now.

TIMETABLES

If you are the type of person who finds time management difficult, whether because you have a near impossible schedule to maintain, or because you are the sort who tends to leave everything to the last minute and then is forced to rush around to get it done, you may find that a timetable is a recurrent image in your dreams. Under these circumstances, your unconscious is prompting you to get organized, prioritize, delegate, or offload some of your duties and generally to make better use of your time.

CLOCKS AND WATCHES

On a practical level, it is not unheard of for the unconscious to act as a timekeeper or to use a dream to jog an individual's memory. This might happen if, for example, in your waking life, you are in danger of forgetting to keep an important appointment that was made some time ago. In this case, your unconscious might remind you of your arrangement in a dream by showing you a clock with the hands pointing to the precise time of that appointment. To dream of a watch whose hands are whizzing round may be reflecting a worry of being late for a meeting or for work. To hear a ticking clock in your dream is a device that brings to mind the passing of time, that tells you literally that

time is "ticking by." Perhaps this is a gentle hint not to waste time but to get things done now, while you can.

CALENDARS

Like clocks, calendars, too, may be used to remind the dreamer of an important date, perhaps a relative's birthday or a rendezvous with a lover. In the latter case, the lover in question may actually be pointing to the very day marked on the page. Or, if the pages are turning, this may be an indicator of the passage of time in a similar manner to the ticking watch, or a suggestion that patience is required, because everything passes in time.

RIVERS OF TIME

An interesting device that the unconscious sometimes employs to make us aware of time is a flowing river. The faster the river flows, the quicker time is passing us by. Conversely, a sluggish flow of water may be advising us not to waste time in our lives lest we miss out on important opportunities.

No time to lose
If our lives are governed by the clock, this will be reflected in our dreams

u n i v e r s a l s y m b o l s

NUMBERS

Numerology, or the study of numbers, is an ancient science based on the belief that numbers correspond to particular forces in nature. Every number emits a pulse, a vibration, each one resonating on a different frequency. In turn, each of these vibrations directly tunes in to one of the patterns or cycles that govern the natural order and rhythm of the universe. No wonder, then, that numbers, which are such important carriers of symbolic meaning, are prominent in all the world's major religious, mythological, and occult traditions.

It all adds up
The significance of dream numbers will depend on what is happening in our daily lives

In his research into dreams, Jung recognized the archetypal energies that are contained in numbers. He saw that in our dreams, by tapping into the collective unconscious (that store of ancient racial memories that we all possess), we are each able to decode the symbolic language of the numbers we see in our dreams, and distill from them their essential power and significance.

But dreams work on many levels, sometimes symbolic, sometimes factual, and sometimes even predictive, so that teasing out the appropriate meaning must be dependent on what is happening in our lives at the time of the dream. Flashing a date on a calendar, for example, may be a reminder of an important occasion. Similarly, someone involved in buying a house may dream of the number on the door of his or her prospective residence. And it is not unheard of for a person to dream the winning numbers of the lottery.

In dreams such as these, the numbers may appear as actual digits, but in others, the significance may lie in clusters of similar objects, such as candles on a birthday cake, or a group of people or row of trees. On a metaphorical level, in whichever guise numbers present themselves, the message will be implicit in their symbolic meaning.

ONE

The number one signifies independence, the leader, or the first. Should this number stand out in your dream, it may be implying that you have the power to stand alone, to succeed, or to win. Alternatively, it can mean the self, as in the expression "number one," and may question your own motives.

TWO

This stands for relationships, duality, or twosomes. This number may be making a comment about you and your partner. Alternatively, two stands for balance, perhaps something you need to strive for in your life.

THREE

The trinity; mind, body, and spirit; the fusion of superego, or ego and id. A symbol of talent, creativity, and self-expression, this number is prompting you to use intuition and imagination to guide you through.

FOUR

Solidity and stability, as in the four equal sides of the square, are implicit in this number. Emphasized in a dream, the number four encourages you to work hard to lay down firm foundations upon which to build your life.

FIVE

The pentagram. Five represents the five senses and inspires you to follow your ambitions, or spread your wings and fly. It can also be an indication that you are about to make an important discovery.

SIX

A stable number that is associated with the family, and with balance and harmony. It symbolizes honesty, integrity, and reliability. The number six in a dream points to trustworthiness.

SEVEN

Associated with mysticism, with religion, and inner wisdom, seven symbolizes inspired writing, poetry, and fine arts. Seven represents the dreamer, the inventor, and those that take the path of solitude.

EIGHT

A lucky number symbolizing wealth – but only wealth earned through dedication, organization, and hard work. Dreaming of number eight may imply that rewards for past efforts are on their way.

NINE

The qualities of humanitarianism, kindness, generosity, and unselfishness are all linked to the number nine. In dreams, it points to an expansion of knowledge through literature and travel.

TEN

The circle, and number of perfection and completion, dreaming of the number ten may confirm the successful outcome of a project or the fulfillment of your dreams.

universal symbols

COLORS

Researchers have shown that most of our dreams are in color. The occasional black-and-white dream, therefore, may be making a statement about the dreamer's vitality or state of mind – a lack of color perhaps implying a draining of stamina or possibly reflecting a bleak outlook. Each individual color carries its own symbolic meaning, so it is particularly significant when one color stands out more prominently than the rest.

Sometimes, the color will be implied by an object – a tomato, an emerald, or a lily, for example, or a personal item in our possession. In these dreams, then, the subconscious mind draws the attention, not so much to the symbolic meaning of the object itself, but to its associated color as in the green of grass, the blue of sky, the yellow of a buttercup or the red of blood.

RED

Red is the universal symbol of passion, both love and rage. Red activates and motivates and therefore denotes energy and vitality. Physiologically, it is associated with the heart and the blood. It corresponds to the first chakra at the base of the spine.

In dreams, it is the color of warmth and stimulation. Depending on your circumstances, it can suggest sexual excitement and desire, anger as in the expression, "a red rag to a bull," or it may be flashing a warning of possible danger.

YELLOW

Yellow is the color of the intellect. Associated with logical processes and communication, it connotes intelligence and verbal dexterity. Yellow is the color of the sun and, according to dream lore, it brings light and laughter into our lives. Corresponding to the third chakra, it works to relieve fear and anxiety and helps to release creative and artistic talents. Yellow in our dreams cheers the spirits, warms the heart, and enlivens the mind.

GREEN

Green is the color of nature, of growth, regeneration, and repair. Green is associated with the notion of renewal, of new life emerging from the old. It is a therapeutic color and to see green in our dreams brings us hope, heals our pain, and restores our balance. Corresponding to the heart chakra, it conveys peace and harmony. Curiously, however, green is also associated with jealousy as in the expression, "green with envy," and also with

Fiery colors

The predominance of yellow and red in this image indicates sexuality and the emotions

naivety. Whichever interpretation applies very much depends on your circumstances at the time of the dream.

BLUE

When blue is emphasized in a dream, its interpretation will depend on the shade that is presented. A vibrant azure, for example, can have you reaching for the skies, as this shade is connected with idealism, aspirations, ambition, and adventure. Mid-blue is calming and concentrates the mind, while deeper blues can lower the spirits to the point of depression. When dark blue predominates in a dream it may be reflecting a somber mood.

Corresponding to the throat chakra, blue promotes introspection and truth in both waking and dream life. Blue is also regarded as the prime healing color.

BLACK AND WHITE

Polar opposites, black is considered negative, symbolizing sadness and loss of hope, while white is a positive color, introducing light, purity, and inspiration. Black recurring in dreams suggests that the dreamer is going through a difficult period in his or her life, and these dreams need to be analyzed carefully. When black predominates in a dream, even the tiniest speck of another color will be significant in bringing a ray of hope and, according to its symbolism, showing a way through. White corresponds to the crown chakra and represents creativity and imagination. Think of white as a clean sheet, thus symbolizing a new beginning. When white features prominently it could mean you will soon "see the light," and find an answer to your problem.

universal symbols

JEWELRY AND GEMSTONES

The preciousness of gems and jewels in real life is matched in our dreams by the symbolic representation of those aspects of our psyches that we value the most – the talent to paint beautiful pictures, compose heavenly music, pen exquisite rhymes, or of priceless characteristics such as truth or beauty, kindness, or a sense of justice and fair play. But also in dreamlore, objects that glitter equally represent our hopes and aspirations, and items that sparkle may symbolize brilliant ideas.

Dreams that feature jewelry may be classed as wish-fulfillment dreams, but if you dream of a broken clasp on an expensive necklace or watch, let's say, it may be a prompt for you to check your own valuables for any damage. Perhaps when you last wore the piece you unconsciously picked up the fact that the catch was loose, but you were in too much of a hurry to register this consciously. Now your dream is playing back this observation, bringing the fault fully to your attention. Taking heed of such warnings could save you a good deal of worry in the long run.

On a symbolic level, to dream that you lose or break an item of jewelry warns of challenges and obstacles ahead. Tarnished jewelry or gems that have lost their sparkle foretell quarrels and disappointment. To be presented with a piece of jewelry suggests that you will soon be rewarded for past efforts, while to find a jewel can either mean that you are about to discover a new talent or that you could be due a lucky windfall.

GOLD AND SILVER

Gold symbolizes wealth, both materially and metaphorically. To dream that you are given a piece of gold suggests that you could soon receive riches, whether in the form of money or in the fulfillment of your desires, such as gaining love, security, self-esteem, peace of mind, or whatever it is that you yearn for in life. Dreaming that you are looking for gold suggests a search for perfection, buying it that you are trying to hide something.

Silver, though not as precious as gold, nevertheless carries a similar message and is especially associated with coinage and therefore with money. Silver, however, is linked to femininity and the moon, and searching for silver in your dreams may be reflecting a need to develop your nurturing potential, or a desire to create something.

To lose either silver or gold in your dream is warning of financial losses, so watch your purse and avoid any risky investments in the next few days.

Vicious rumor

Earrings in dreams draw attention to what you are hearing: perhaps news or gossip

GEMSTONES

It has long been recognized that individual stones each carry a symbolic meaning of their own. Occasionally, however, the message of the dream lies not in the stone itself but in its color. Correct interpretation regarding this will depend on the dreamer's life circumstances at the time of the dream.

Diamonds represent victory; emeralds symbolize good fortune; rubies foretell visitors. Opinion is divided as far as pearls are concerned. Some experts maintain that, because a pearl is shaped like a teardrop, it bodes sadness. Others, however, mindful of the saying, "pearls of wisdom," believe them to bring good luck.

RINGS

Eternal symbols of love that, when given to you in a dream, augur a happy relationship. But to lose a golden ring warns that emotional problems could be brewing.

EARRINGS

Earrings draw the attention to the ear, so this dream concerns news and information. Depending on your circumstances, it might be implying that you need to listen more carefully to those around you, or it may be an omen of good news heading your way. If your earrings are tarnished or if you happen to lose one, it could be a warning that malicious gossip is discrediting your good name.

NECKLACES AND BRACELETS

Necklaces and bracelets that are studded with jewels may symbolize your accomplishments and your achievements in life. These augur well as a comment on your feelings of self-esteem. However, do beware if these items resemble chains, especially so if made of a base metal, as this implies that you are feeling tied down or "chained" to your duties and responsibilities. If the necklace has a large stone attached, this might be the proverbial "millstone around your neck," or a bracelet might develop into manacles.

LAST WORDS

Those of us who have problems to solve or important decisions to make would do well to remember the words of our wise grandmothers who would invariably counsel us to "sleep on it." Such advice may indeed have been offered as a palliative, intended to soothe our troubled minds or to prevent hasty action that we might subsequently come to regret. And yet this advice is not as fatuous as it may sound, for sleeping on a problem is a technique that has not only been practised, but has been actively encouraged, by different civilizations throughout the world for thousands of years. The technique is known as "incubating a dream."

Essentially, it involves asking your unconscious to come up with an answer. And usually it does – in dream form. Experiencing the dream itself is the first part. It means that you are in touch with your unconscious, that you can programme yourself to reach the depths of your understanding, to access information stored in the labyrinthine passageways of your memory. It means that you are freely able to dip into the bottomless pool of the collective unconscious, to put together into a coherent picture your daytime misgivings, your hopes, joys, aims, and desires, to highlight your intuitive hunches and to emerge with insights that not only help to address your present situation, but also enhance your very experience of life itself.

The second part is in decoding the dream, or learning to understand the language in which the answer is phrased. And interpreting this all-important expression of your unconscious mind is what *The Dream Catcher* has attempted to teach you to do for yourself. It is hoped, you have learned to trust your own intuition, to believe in your own judgment, to have faith in your own wisdom.

Carl Jung believed that we dream all the time – through the day as well as through the night. According to him, the essential difference between sleeping and waking is that during the day our conscious processes disrupt our ability to access our unconscious thoughts.

Only by introducing an element of crossover – learning to spill our dreams into our days and to take our daily reasoning into our nightly reveries – can we unravel the depths of our understanding and find the key that enables us, at will, to unlock the full creative potential of both our sleeping and waking minds.

May all your dreams enlighten your days

INDEX

ACKNOWLEDGEMENTS

The publishers are grateful to the following for permission to reproduce pictures

Bridgeman Art Library: pp 2, 8, 10, 16, 18, 23, 27, 28, 29, 30, 35, 52, 54, 55, 56, 58, 59, 61, 66, 67, 68, 69, 72, 75, 76, 77, 78, 79, 80, 81l, 97, 98, 100, 101, 103, 105, 106, 107, 109, 110, 113, 115, 121, 123

e.t. archive: 3, 11, 19, 20, 33, 34, 36, 38, 40, 44, 62, 64, 65, 73, 74, 81r, 94, 96, 102, 112, 114

ZEFA picture library: 57, 59, 63, 70, 71, 82, 83, 85, 86, 87, 89, 91, 92, 93

Studio photography by Ian Parsons

Illustrations by Ivan Hissey and Grace Crivellaro

Dream catchers made by Grace Crivellaro

Picture research by Vanessa Fletcher